The Art of Self-Coaching:
How to Understand, Grow, Learn, & Thrive

by Nick Trenton
www.NickTrenton.com

Table of Contents

THE ART OF SELF-COACHING: HOW TO UNDERSTAND, GROW, LEARN, & THRIVE

TABLE OF CONTENTS

CHAPTER 1. FRAMEWORKS FOR CHANGE

ROAD 1: THE GROW MODEL
STEP 1: GOALS
STEP 2: REALITY
STEP 3: OPTIONS
STEP 4: WILL
ROAD 2: THE OUTCOME FRAME MODEL

CHAPTER 2. KNOW YOURSELF, GROW YOURSELF

THE WHEEL OF LIFE
THE 6 BASIC HUMAN NEEDS
LOVE AND CONNECTION
VARIETY
SIGNIFICANCE
CERTAINTY
GROWTH
CONTRIBUTION
UNDERSTANDING YOUR VALUES
WHAT ABOUT MY GOALS?
VALUE CLARIFICATION, STEP BY STEP
VISUALIZING YOUR FUTURE SELF

CHAPTER 3. THE POWER OF OBJECTIVITY

SELF-AWARENESS QUESTIONS
HOW TO OBSERVE YOURSELF
SHINING A LIGHT ON YOUR BLIND SPOTS
THE JOHARI WINDOW TECHNIQUE
QUESTIONS FOR EACH STAGE OF YOUR JOURNEY
CLARITY QUESTIONS
PURPOSE QUESTIONS
CHALLENGE QUESTIONS
ACTION QUESTIONS
GETTING-UNSTUCK QUESTIONS

CHAPTER 4. ATTITUDE IS DESTINY

EMBRACE THE PAIN OF SELF-DISCIPLINE
GRANT YOURSELF PERMISSION
CHANGE TAKES VULNERABILITY
THE EGO CAN JEOPARDIZE GROWTH
TECHNIQUE 1: SEEK OUT FAILURE
TECHNIQUE 2: REFRAME WHAT IT MEANS TO BE CHALLENGED

SUMMARY GUIDE

Chapter 1. Frameworks for Change

Let's begin this book with a question: how does anyone go from point A to point B?

If you're physically traveling from place to place, you'll need a vehicle. But arguably if you're traveling from one state of being to another, you'll also need a vehicle. Whenever we make a real change in who we are, how we behave, what we feel and how we think, we are essentially transforming from one way of being into another.

We can get to where we want to go in many ways, by using many different vehicles. The vehicle often depends on the goal. We could try psychotherapy or ask a mentor to show us the ropes in a new industry. We could go to university or sign up for a personal development course. We could ask our parents!

But did you notice anything in common with these "vehicles"? They're all driven by someone else.

When you form a relationship with a teacher, mentor, counsellor, advisor, guru, consultant, or expert, you are attempting to get from point A to B with the help and guidance of someone else. It's like looking out for a bus going to the place you want to go, or hopping in a taxi and telling the taxi driver where you need to be.

When you hire a coach of any kind, you are not engaging in therapy or consulting, and the coach never tells you what to do, but engages you in a conversation, asks you questions, and helps you figure out what you're trying to achieve. They are assuming a certain amount of responsibility and self-knowledge on your part – they know that you have it in you, but you need the space and support to help you access that "it," whatever it may be. But, to extend the driving metaphor as far as it can go, you can drive yourself. You can give this same space and support to *yourself*, and trust you have it in you, whatever the "it" may be.

Self-coaching is nothing more than a way to instigate and support meaningful changes in your own life, and under your own steam. A way to drive yourself from point A to point B.

Conventional coaching is a great model for personal development, but it has drawbacks. It's expensive, and you may find yourself having serious incompatibilities with your chosen coach (and by "incompatibilities" I also mean that some coaches are just not particularly good!). Think of it this way: in a coaching session, a coach may see where you are, understand the obstacle in your way, and prompt you with a question to bring insight and spur a change in your behavior. The desired change in behavior isn't just superficial or external, though – it has to arise from some internal change. And if that change comes from within you, then the coach was only ever instrumental. They didn't *make* you change. You changed yourself.

Good coaching is about:

- Creating the right space and opportunity for change and growth
- Reflecting on your process and developing your sense of being a proactive agent in that process
- Developing self-awareness
- Learning to trial-and-error your own behavior, and experimenting with your experience
- Practicing ways of finding help and community with others
- Bravely confronting your limiting beliefs and thought patterns and challenging your mental models so you can rebuild your life from the inside out

Looking at this list, there is no reason you do none of this for yourself. The benefit of a coach is that they are a separate person, standing outside of you, able to (hopefully) supply you with objective feedback about what's going on in your world. But, with self-awareness, honesty, and enough discipline to be consistent, you can step outside of your world in exactly the same way, and look at it objectively, just as a coach would.

A coach can give structure to your process, and bring your attention to things you may have been mindless about before. They can call out all your blind spots and challenge you when they think you're ready. Is it possible to do this for yourself? Yes!

Just remember that change, whenever it happens, is first an internal, personal event. Growth, if it occurs, does so because the person doing the growing had within them everything that was needed. We can encourage a seed to grow into the best tree it can be, but the seed always "knows" how to be a tree, and can be nothing else, whether we were there to help it or not. Similarly, right now as you read this book, remind yourself that you possess a powerful inner drive towards development. In the same way as you are alive doing nothing special to make it happen, you also possess a spirit of growth and development within you. This allows you to drive yourself.

This spirit can be wasted, misused or twisted out of shape. Just because a person can drive a car, it doesn't mean they can do it perfectly without ever getting driving lessons! With a conscious goal and with effort, we can shape and support our innate drive towards growth so it can best fulfill its potential. Self-coaching can encompass all sorts of techniques and approaches, including ritual, journaling, setting goals, running thought experiments, practicing mindfulness, and engaging in Socratic dialogue… with yourself.

All these techniques, however, are about working with your inbuilt capacity for growth. In the chapters that follow, we'll be exploring these techniques, but it is not a *directive*. These are not rules or commands, but a framework to help you organize your journey as you drive from A to B. We'll explore all the things we need to grow:

1. Awareness of where we are and where we want to go
2. The tools to get us there
3. Enough objectivity to gain feedback and see how we're doing

4. A sensible framework to put it all together (for example, something like this book!)

Let's dive in.

Road 1: The GROW Model

One thing that will become immediately obvious when you embark on a personal development mission is this: you have choices. Nobody is coming to *tell* you which the right way is to go – it's your job to ask questions, act consciously, and take responsibility for the outcomes. The first big fork in the road is to choose which framework makes the most sense for you. The big idea here is: there is no "right" way – there is only what works. And only you can say if it works.

One path you can take, i.e., one way you can organize your developmental process, is called the GROW model. First created by Sir John Whitmore and his colleagues in the 80s, the model was outlined in a book, *Coaching for Performance*, which quickly became a bestseller. The model outlines a structure for a coaching session, and breaks down sequential steps that bring you closer to solutions. It goes like this:

GOAL: What do you want?

REALITY: What is happening now?

OPTIONS: What can you do?

WILL: What will you do?

This process happens any time we develop, but if we consciously and proactively engage with it, it becomes a powerful tool. If you get stuck, come back to this framework for clarity. If you feel overwhelmed or unhappy, come back to the framework to focus on the solution, rather than the problem. The steps are clear and in order, so you won't wander off too far from what ultimately matters: being consciously aware of what you have now (point A), what you want (point B), and how you can get there (travel the distance between them). In this way, self-coaching differs greatly from open-ended reflection or therapy – you always tether your insights back to concrete action.

Let's look at each step with examples.

Step 1: Goals

So, what do you want anyway? Seems simple but so much is jeopardized at this first step, when we only *think* we have set ourselves goals, when we have nothing more than vague and ill-defined wishes and hopes. To simply be "better" is not enough. What does that actually look like? When you're outlining your goals, ask yourself these questions, remembering that a goal that is crisp and clear is the one most likely to happen for you:

When do you want your goal to materialize? Remember that goals look different depending on their time scales

What are the details of this goal? Outline your specific thoughts, feelings and behaviors.

What is your goal, stated simply and in words?

How will you know when you've actually achieved it?

What kind of goal is this – something you have? Something you are? Something you do?

What's the point of this goal, i.e., what are the benefits?

How will life be different after the goal? How will you be different?

By asking yourself these questions, you take nothing for granted. Don't assume that your goals are obvious! And don't assume that just because a goal seems appealing or necessary at first, that you'll ultimately choose it. It's common, for example, for people to unconsciously adopt the goals of those around them, which might align with their own, deep down. It would be a shame to discover this only after you've spent time and effort achieving something that's not actually meaningful for you!

For a simple example, imagine that you are in high school and thinking about your future. Everyone in your family has gone to university, including all your older siblings, and the assumption is that you will, too. They've all studied medicine or done degrees in biology or chemistry, and your teachers all agree these subjects are your strengths, too. But somewhere along the way, you need to figure out what *you* want.

Like many teenagers, you're not yet sure who you are or what you want your life to look like. Following the GOAL model, you work hard to clarify your goals. But every time you try, you can't seem to visualize yourself at university, doing medicine. You can't picture the benefits. The vision seems hazy in your mind, and you're neither inspired nor challenged at the thought. As you can see, the Goal part of the process can not only help you identify new goals, but clarify and question old ones. After a while, maybe you realize something important: that you don't want to study medicine, and you don't actually want to go to university.

You sit down and ask yourself more deeply *what do I want?* You notice you are more excited and focused on a different goal: starting your own business. This becomes so real in your mind you can almost taste it. You state the goal clearly: you want to complete training to be an electrician, while working as an apprentice, and then within two years work for yourself as an independent contractor. You can see this end-point: you feel competent and proud, and you're making enough money to support yourself. You can see the steps to get there. You can even see your business cards, printed with your name on them, and can imagine yourself picking them up from the printers. Your goal is no longer vague, meaningless or uninspiring (such as the goal: "go to university and study some sort of medicine thing and then, I don't know, find a job I guess?") but razor-sharp.

This clarity, this ability to *see*, is what the first step is all about. You'll know you're ready to move to the next step when you feel this clarity, and are itching to bring it to life.

Step 2: Reality

But what about Point A? Your ability to get to Point B depends on the limits and resources you can find in Point A. The thing about asking "what is happening right now?" is that you discover there are many things happening, and many perspectives to take. Get a good sense of your world as it is right now. The "before" to your "after"!

What is the situation currently?

How far away from your goal are you?

How do you think and feel about the situation (i.e., how are you in the present)?

What have you tried so far? What has worked and what hasn't?

What are you doing to bring about your goal? Is it working?

What are the obstacles?

What resources do you have access to?

How does the current situation affect you and others right now?

Whatever you do, don't rush this step. It's uncomfortable to dwell on the present if all you want to do is escape it. Some life coaches would unknowingly encourage a kind of denial, and would repeatedly draw your attention to all the positive things that are possible. But without a clear understanding of what *is*, you're not able to fully understand what *could be*.

Engaging with reality is not about dwelling on the problem, though. Negative self-talk can distract us from the process. For example, we start to say, "this is hopeless,

I'm a failure" instead of, "my current situation isn't working for me." The difference is an attitude of calm neutrality focusing on the present with *an intention of finding solutions, rather than making judgments.*

Watch yourself closely as you engage this step, and make sure you're not rushing from the past to the future, and skipping right over the present. For example, you might say, "she cheated, and I told her to move out. I'm going to file for divorce and that's that." But doing so hides the present moment – how do you feel right now? Events and feelings from the past are being allowed to dictate future actions. But if so, you never give yourself the chance to gain a new perspective in the present, and act from that. You could say instead, "she cheated, and I told her to move out. We're both feeling pretty hurt and confused right now. I'm taking the weekend to think things over and then we're having a discussion on Monday to talk about a way forward."

When things are difficult, there is a temptation to rush to action, and to consider options. It can feel wrong to *not* make a pronouncement or come to a conclusion or decision as soon as possible. But give yourself time to develop more awareness of the situation. Insights may come – but they need time and space. They need for you to cool off and consider other perspectives.

You can act from the emotional energy that comes with rehashing stories about the past, or you can act from the calm that comes from neutrally considering the present, as it is now. Usually, acting from the emotional momentum of the past keeps you in confusion. You are merely being reactive. But if you cool off first and observe yourself with awareness, you become firm in your resolve, and proactive.

In our example, rushing to sign divorce papers comes from an immediate sense of betrayal and anger, and shuts us out to the realities in the present. If we explore the present, however, we might see we are not as angry now as we were yesterday. We can see the impact of the event on us right now – and how this is evolving with time. We can explore new possible realities without being rash. When we feel like our awareness has grown and that we have a new level of insight or understanding (i.e., we know something now that we didn't before), we are ready to move to the next level, where we translate insight into action.

Step 3: Options

Once you feel a new energy and clarity around the issue, you will naturally wonder about actions to move you forwards. We should only consider options for action once we've planned out our goal and have a full grasp of the reality in front of us.

What is possible here?

What can you do in this situation?

What are the steps and actions available to you?

How can you learn more about doing things right?

How might other people act in your shoes?

If there were no limits, what would you do?

What related actions have worked well for you in the past?

This step is the step of possibility, so keep things as open-ended as you can. Brainstorm ideas. Don't be in too much of a hurry to nail down one action. You can do this by continuing to ask, "is there anything else?" after you come up with a possibility. Keep asking yourself this until you run out of ideas, or you find yourself repeating things.

Useful options often stem from insight and understanding gained in the previous step. For example, you might have learned of the fact that you always fail in your exercise resolutions because you hate going to the gym. Without this insight, you would just barge ahead with the goal of going to the gym more. If you do steps 2 and 3 fully, though, you realize that you can be more active by doing something you already know you enjoy – walking your dog, playing sports, dancing or hiking.

Step 4: Will

It should be a seamless flow from option to action.

What are you going to do?

How?

When?

With whom?

What's the way forward?

How shall I wrap up?

When you reach this step, a lack of commitment or clarity is a signal you might benefit from doing the GROW process again to uncover any blocks or limits. Comfortably feel the full force of your will here; if not, don't worry – just reiterate the previous steps until you do. Don't act *unless* you feel you have enough clarity and determination to do so. For example, you may be deliberating over how to deal with increasing dissatisfaction in your job, and decide after long reflection you want to search for a new one. You'll know you've completed the process when the thought of handing in your resignation letter "feels right" – it feels like a solution and a way forward.

Road 2: The Outcome Frame Model

But remember, the GROW framework is just that – a framework. The "outcome frame model" takes you to the same place as the GROW model; it just takes a slightly different route to get there. As a framework, it has a lot in common with the GROW model, and it guides you step-by-step through achieving what you set out to achieve.

To use this framework, you first create what is called an Outcome Frame. Here, you create your Desired State and remove all the obstacles in the way to you achieving that state. You simultaneously stir up excitement and inspiration for the Desired State. It's like doing whatever you can to step off the brake pedal while stepping more on the accelerator pedal.

An underlying principle to the approach is that "human beings always choose the best available feeling on the menu." This means that while people naturally want to optimize – everyone wants to feel better – we can always improve this process by increasing our range of perceived options. We add more choices to the menu. So, the technique is two-fold:

1. Remove obstacles

2. Take the freed up energy from pushing against those obstacles and point it towards the Desired State

Much like our previous model, we discover what we want, we clarify how we will get it, and we conclude by acting. The difference here is that Desired State can mean quite a lot of things and encompass internal or psychological changes. Second, this model puts a little more focus on what change/evolution will cost you, your roadblocks, and how you'll get through them.

Let's look at the steps:

Step 1: Identify what you want. Define your Desired State

Step 2: Identify the benefits of achieving that state, and what it will feel and look like for you

Step 3: Identify the criteria for knowing you've achieved it

Step 4: What are the side effects, costs, and risks? Identify what valuable thing you must let go of to achieve your Desired State

Step 5: Identify the context and details of the Desired State – who, when, where, how

Step 6: Identify the next steps you can take

As you can see, it's the same journey we identified above, it just takes a different route, with a few more pitstops. Here's how you might use this idea in practice:

Step 1: You decide you want to lose 10 pounds

Step 2: You imagine the benefits – you'll look and feel better, you'll be healthier, you'll feel proud of yourself, and you'll be able to better enjoy your favorite activities and hobbies. You envision yourself feeling lighter on your feet, and more confident. In your mind's eye, you even picture yourself wearing a new outfit you look amazing in. You feel great.

Step 3: You'll know you've achieved your goal when the scale records 10 pounds gone!

Step 4: There's a lot you must give up. For one, your excuses. You'll have to stop being passive and blaming other things for your habits and lifestyle, and you'll have to get a handle on emotional overeating and being lazy about working out. Plus, you'll have to give up eating so much junk food! There are costs and risks – it takes energy, strategy and willpower to stick to a weight loss plan, and it's way more comfortable to just do nothing. Also, there's a risk of failing and feeling worse about yourself instead of better. You have to have faith in yourself, and that can feel like a gamble!

Step 5: Here's where you outline the details of so-called SMART goals. You give yourself the specific and realistic goal of losing 10 pounds, within one month. You also identify the context of this achievement – you note the people that could help you (a weight loss mentor, a nutritionist or trainer, your spouse), the time and place (you'll weigh yourself every 3 days, after your shower and before breakfast at 8 am) and the weight loss approach you'll be using (10,000 steps a day combined with a fixed daily caloric reduction during the month).

Step 6: Seeing all this, you, at last, identify the next step you can take. This could be throwing out tempting snack foods, contacting a trainer or nutritionist, heading to the grocery store to stock up on veggies, or announcing to everyone your intentions, so they hold you accountable. It's great if your actions concretely connect to your obstacles and work to remove them.

The above steps are designed to be mulled over all at once. The recommendation is that you sit for 15 minutes at a minimum to strategize, and you'll know you're done when you have a concrete set of actions to get you started. The above example is pretty simple, but this approach can be used for all sorts of goals. The Desired State can be anything – attitudes, actions, realizations, feelings, or events. It's usually best, however, to break big goals down into smaller ones, just for clarity's sake.

What if you sit down to create an Outcome Frame and you get stuck at the first step, i.e., you have no idea what you want? This isn't a problem. We usually do this exercise when we have a clear idea that we need to do *something*, but we're not yet clear on the details and are lacking direction. Your problem may be that you know what you want but don't have a plan for how to get it, or maybe you aren't even clear on what you desire. We can sometimes land up here when we've been sitting with a problem for a long time and have lost the ability to even imagine a way out. We can also find ourselves here if we've succumbed to negative self-talk and repeatedly placed our attention on the problem, almost forgetting there could ever be a solution.

If this is you, a good idea is to start with what you *don't* want. Really flesh it out in your imagination. But don't just stop there or dwell on the negatives. Switch your *un*want around and look at its opposite. This may show you your real desires.

Steps 1, 2, and 3 are a little like the Goals stage in the GROW model, where we identify our goals and imagine them vividly. Step 4, where we identify roadblocks, is akin to perceiving reality in the second step of the GROW model. Options and Will are similar to step 4 and 5, respectively.

Where these models differ is in the importance they assign to each step. There is more focus in GROW on fully engaging with the present reality, whereas in the Outcome Frame model, you are asked to perceive only the roadblocks, risks and costs in the present moment. This means you may skip over new potentials or untapped resources. The Outcome Frame model also asks you to consider the details of your chosen goal in step 5, where you think about the context and the who, what, where and why. But unlike the GROW model, you are not considering *all* feasible options, just those of the path you've already identified. While the GROW model does allow you to do this, it lacks the Outcome Frame's focus on what frequently derails any growth attempt: resistance.

Two approaches, two sets of advantages and disadvantages. As we said in the beginning of this chapter, this book is not about telling you which approach is "right", but acknowledging that we have the option to choose an approach that fits us best, depending on our needs.

Consider using the GROW approach if:

- You're trying to problem-solve, think out of the box or uncover a novel solution via a perspective switch or paradigm shift

- You are at the start of a journey, and want to clarify an overall strategy
- Your goal is more *external*: i.e., more action-based, practical, creative or involving others

Consider using the Outcome Frame model if:

- Your goals are more internal: i.e., personal, psychological or relational
- You have tried to change before and failed, i.e., certain mental obstacles cause resistance, and you need to address that
- You are already on a previously chosen path but need to fine-tune your process

One way to move forward is to use *both* processes. Start with the GROW approach at first, then use the Outcome Frame model to keep tabs on yourself, and do regular "maintenance" on your overall strategy. While the GROW process is done sequentially, and each step only commences when the previous step is finished, the Outcome Frame approach is done all at once, in around 15 minutes.

You might blend the two using the best of both. Sit down and create an Outcome Frame, but import sections from the GROW model. In our weight loss example, this might mean inserting an extra step before step 5, where you tease apart the goal's details. Take the time to first consider different options and possibilities for achieving your goal, so you know you're not rushing ahead with something that will ultimately fail. You might do this and discover that calorie counting is a big disaster for you, since it only draws your attention to what you can't eat, and makes you feel deprived. But by exploring your options in an open-ended way first, you can discover this is not the only option. There are many other ways to lose weight; you could try intermittent fasting instead, for example.

You could stick mainly with the GROW model but include a thorough assessment of your own resistance in step two, Reality. For example, when you're asking the question, "what is happening right now?" you could remember to include internal, psychological factors, too, such as "I seem to keep self-sabotaging" or "apparently I can never be trusted around Oreos."

Long story short: you can do what you like. Remember, you're in the driver's seat! It's not worth getting too hung up on *which* framework you use, since each will have virtues and drawbacks. Rather, it matters *how* you're using a framework, and whether it's doing the job you want it to do. Is it making it easier for you to travel from point A to point B? It's better to use a framework you like, but it is infinitely preferable to use a flawed framework than to have no framework. Why not create one yourself?

To grow and evolve we need only self-awareness, a clear perception of possibilities and obstacles, tools that work, and a practical, action-based plan to create the world we want to create. Exactly how we negotiate the details will depend heavily on who we are, and what we are trying to achieve.

And this is precisely the theme of our next chapter.

Summary:

- A coach facilitates our growth process, but that doesn't mean we cannot coach ourselves. With self-awareness, a framework for change, the right tools, and the ability to be objective about our progress, we can help ourselves achieve our goals.
- Change occurs when we move from Point A to Point B. There are many ways to cover that distance, but you'll need a framework to help you organize yourself.
- One useful model of change is the coaching model called GROW, in which the letters spell Goals (what do I want?), Reality (what is happening right now?), Options (what could I do?) and Will (what will I do?). We will see these essential steps repeated all throughout the remainder of the book.
- Another model is the Outcome Frame model, which asks us to take concrete steps towards achieving our Desired State, i.e., goal.

- Step 1: Identify what you want. Define your Desired State. We identify what we want, and understand the benefits of that change, and the criteria for measuring its success. We also consider all the obstacles to our achieving this goal, and iron out the exact details and context. Finally, we end in a comparable way to the GROW model: we take concrete action.
- There is no right or wrong framework, but the GROW model may work better for professional or external goals, whereas The Outcome Frame model may be better for more personal or relationship goals.

Chapter 2. Know Yourself, Grow Yourself

We've talked about growth, development, and evolution as though these ideas always meant the same things to all people at all times. Finding a job may be a successful endpoint for one person... but quitting an identical job is considered a success for another. The same choice could be an expression of resistance for person A but a sign of deep insight and transformation for person B. And even within the same person, the definition of growth seems to change, so what seemed an all-important achievement at 20 years of age seems insignificant at 40.

There are no objectively "good" choices, life paths or outcomes. What matters is the degree of fit between a unique individual and the goals they've chosen for themselves, i.e., is it good *for you*. We all want to fulfil our potential. We all want to be better today than we were yesterday, and we all want to improve and progress. But what that looks like depends on who we are. So, we need to clarify the answers to 2 important questions:

What do we want?
Who are we?

In this chapter, we'll see these are essentially the same question! To understand what we want, we need to know who we are. And to better know who we are, we need to explore the things we want. We've looked at frameworks, now it's time to look at the goals we want to set, and the changes we want to bring about in our lives. Think of it this way: the framework is just a map. We still need to chart our own unique course through this map, in a chosen direction, to a chosen destination.

Many people are experts at personal development techniques and methods, but it doesn't seem to matter because they are not using these methods in service of an appropriate and well-chosen goal. Finding the goal (i.e., the direction of growth) that matters to you is the subject of this chapter.

The Wheel of Life

Not quite sure what you want? That's OK!

Let's start from the beginning, by using a popular tool called the Wheel of Life, which was created by Paul J Meyer in the 60s, and is loosely inspired by an older version that comes from Tibetan Buddhist philosophy. Life can be broken down into eight segments or areas, laid out on a wheel. The wheel can be used to home in on goals because it invites you to carefully reflect on where you are right now in your life, regarding each segment.

Considering each area, think about how much time and attention you spend on each, and your overall satisfaction and achievement. The 8 aspects are:

Business and career
Finances
Health

Family and friends
Romance
Personal development
Fun and recreation
Contribution to society

Imagine that life is a giant pie divided into the above 8 slices. To use the pie, you can assign each slice a value from 1 to 10, to represent your development in this area. The value of 1 (representing the least satisfaction or achievement) is nearest the center of the pie, with 10 (representing the most) at the circumference. The result resembles a bullseye or set of 10 concentric circles. You can find blank templates of the wheel of life online, or you can easily sketch your own.

Now, look at each segment and mark its score. Maybe you decide finances are iffy and mark this 4, but mark romance as a 10, and so on. It's important to take your time and fill this out as honestly as you can. You are not assigning a score according to how important you think this category is, but giving an honest appraisal of how well you're fulfilling challenges, how much you've achieved, and how satisfied you are with this part of life. It can be a shock to realize that even though you *claim* that friends and family are important, for instance, you nevertheless score poorly.

When you're done, join all the dots up. Get something that looks like a spider web. Take a moment to just look at the whole picture. You should immediately be able to get a sense of what lacks your life, and what is working well. Seeing things all together at a glance like this allows you to visualize life's overall balance. Maybe you have a relatively even circle – but it's small and hovering at the 4 or 5 mark. Or maybe you have a very jagged and pointy shape, suggesting that your energies and attentions are unevenly divided across the different areas of life.

Let's look at how an imaginary person might complete such a wheel:

Business and career
8 – I'm satisfied with my job, and I feel like it's a good match for my skills. I can see opportunities for growth in the next few years. I'm proud of my occupation.

Finances
10 – Salary is really good! I'm saving well and feel comfortable.

Health
3 – I'm honestly in pretty bad shape. Not happy with my overall weight. I'm still smoking, and I'm getting concerned about my lungs.

Family and friends
5 – This is ticking along but it could be better. Feeling kind of distant from family right now, and I've been feeling alienated in my friendship group for some time now.

Romance
6 – Married 8 years, so what romance, right? I love my wife. We kind of take each other for granted, though. There's a lot of trust, but I wouldn't say we enjoy one another anymore.

Personal development
7 – Pretty good. Doing therapy once a week and I feel like I'm making interesting headway with some stuff from the past.

Fun and recreation
2 – My life isn't fun at all. I never relax. There's no time for hobbies because I'm always working.

Contribution to society
1 – This one is the hardest one to think about. I love my job but let's be honest, it's not making the world a better place. I'm not sure what I'm ultimately meant to be doing with my life, and what impact I make on the bigger picture. I earn a lot, but I never donate to charity, and I feel awful about that. I'd feel much less isolated in life if I knew I was part of something bigger.

What you may notice is this exercise is subjective. For example, the question, "are you satisfied with your health?" depends on how you define health, and what your standards are. If you're an ultra-buff health enthusiast, you might rate your health a 4 simply because you had an injury that prevented you from training for a week. But if you're recovering from cancer, the fact that you are in remission and finally have hair after chemo may be enough for you to rate your health as 10! Both ratings are right.

You may amend this wheel a little to reflect the values you already know you hold. You could combine categories (maybe you're an activist who considers "contribution" and "career" as one) or add them (maybe you're 90 years old and want to get rid of "romance" and include another category, "spirituality.")

But, however you divide this pie, consider this. You only have a finite amount of energy, of time, of *life*. How are you allocating this amount to the different areas? In our example above, it would be clear after the exercise this person needs to channel some energy into making life more meaningful (by contributing to society) and more fun. Their focus on work is probably negatively influencing their health, relationships, and overall sense of life purpose, even though work is fulfilling. By doing the exercise, however, he can see not only how each area measures up, but also how these areas interact and relate. He can see that his life is unbalanced.

Ask yourself, what exactly made your low scores low? What seems to work and what doesn't? At a glance, how could you achieve more balance?

Once you notice patterns, the next step will become obvious: you need to act. The point of this exercise is self-knowledge, but ultimately this self-knowledge is used to inspire useful action. What's more, when you return to your wheel of life, say, 6 months later, you can also use it as a tool to track and monitor your development. How well did your actions work? Come back to the drawing board and strategize again.

Taking a life snapshot in this way is not going to reveal in-depth insights about your true nature, but it will show you how each area of life relates to each other area. It will show you where change most likely needs to occur first. And it will also show you everything that you're doing right!

The 6 Basic Human Needs

Let's look at things another way. We can learn more about who we are, and what we want to achieve with our lives, by looking closely at what we *need*. Seedlings need sunlight and water to be happy – well, what do humans need to be happy? But this question has been a perennial favorite with psychologists for a long time. In fact, we could see our very desire for creating a meaningful and purpose-driven life as a need in itself.

If we have what we need, we will feel happy, successful, and fulfilled. If we don't, we won't. So, what are these special human needs? The most common list contains six:

Love and connection
Variety
Significance
Certainty
Growth
Contribution

It's claimed that the first 4 are necessary for survival, but all 6 are required for a richer, more gratifying life. Let's look closely.

Love and connection
We all need to feel we are a part of something bigger than ourselves. It's human nature to want to relate to one another, to

connect and communicate, to give and receive, to be valued and seen, and to bond. "Love" can manifest in countless forms, from the closeness we feel for family, to romantic love, to our friendships, and even to basic touch and eye contact. We can find our sense of human connection in marriages and relationships, clubs and groups, religions, pets, praise and recognition, sex, being cared for, raising children, charity, and much more. One thing we seem unable to do is live without it!

Just because something is a fundamental human need, though, it doesn't mean that every expression will be positive or healthy. We can find belonging in gangs or toxic relationships, and we can feel seen when we bully and dominate others. We can be promiscuous or play the victim to convince others to care for us, or replace human affection with several addictions.

Variety

You may be surprised to see this listed as a human need, but only consider how much depression and unhappiness seem to resemble being stuck in a rut. We all need to live in a rich and stimulating environment. Change is part of life – in many ways, change *is* life, and when nothing ever changes, it can feel like things are, almost literally, dead.

We all indeed vary in the size of our appetite for variety, but even the most routine-bound and predictable person wants to try something new now and again! Heathy ways to meet this need include travel, new foods, new hobbies, or learning. Unhealthy ways include self-harm, risk-taking behavior, substance abuse or "creating drama."

Think of your physical muscles – if you don't move and stretch them, they become stiff, weak, and prone to injury. Similarly, if we don't use the full range of our psychological, emotional or spiritual bodies, we are sorely missing out.

Humans come alive when there's challenge, novelty and a little surprise. We need to feel fun and excitement, but also a little risk. We need to experiment. Wherever your threshold is, monotony and boredom are serious threats to your overall wellbeing.

You'll be like the sad panda at the zoo in a concrete enclosure, with every day exactly the same as every other day.

Significance

Humans have always asked what the meaning of life is, but perhaps what we most want to know is that *we* have meaning, at least to someone. Humans need to feel important, needed and wanted. It needs to feel like we have a place here in the world, and that we'd be missed if we were not here. Sadly, our culture is rife with dominance hierarchies and comparisons that can demolish self-esteem, and many people do suffer a deep yearning to feel more significant. Instead, we may feel small and unworthy, like our hopes and dreams are trivial, like we are invisible... or just plain old not special.

The healthy way to satisfy this normal human need is to genuinely provide something of value (sounds like "contribution to society" doesn't it?). This could be creating art, building something useful, serving others, taking a stance, caring for your family, creating wealth and success, or cultivating spiritual maturity. Unhealthy ways include tearing down others so you can feel big, "acting out" for attention or being narcissistic and boastful.

Certainty
Safety, comfort, and predictability. Humans want to avoid pain and fear, and feel that their world is stable, secure and grounded. Not knowing where your next meal is coming from, not knowing what you're doing next Tuesday, or not knowing what you're doing with your life in general – these things can stress a person out and cause unhappiness. Again, though, it's a matter of preference and personality. Some of us are a little more comfortable tolerating the unknown and the unpredictable, whereas others need a lot of safety and predictability to feel OK.

We can satisfy this need in ongoing relationships, friendships, and family, and by seeking to build financial security for ourselves. A safe home, a routine, and a certain trust with people and things around you will provide certainty. This need can be improperly fed, however, by hoarding and bingeing behavior, or the obsessive need to control. When we complain, micromanage others or act clingy, we are also meeting the need for certainty in a less-than-ideal way.

You might be wondering, "wait, isn't this need the opposite of the need for variety?" Well, yes. Humans are complex! We each have our own optimal balance between opposing needs, requiring safety and security – but not so much it becomes stifling.

Growth
In this chapter, we're looking at fulfilling our needs to support growth. But growth itself is a need. The desire to develop and mature is probably what made you pick up this book. Change is continuous, and we all change throughout our different life stages. A human who is not growing, learning, adapting, and maturing is not much of a human! If we stop, our physical, cognitive, emotional, and spiritual capacities will wither and atrophy.

Each of us needs to know that our experiences amount to something, that we are growing closer and closer towards something better than what we are now. Human life – and all life – wants to expand. We can fulfil this need by constantly challenging ourselves and supporting our learning and practice, whatever our chosen field. We can gain wisdom, skill and knowledge. We can feel like our mistakes mean something since they taught us how to be better. If we satisfy this need in an unhealthy way, though, we may get distracted by behaviors or ideas that merely feel like progress, but aren't. We may make up excuses... and start believing them!

Contribution
Finally, this is the need to go beyond one's own narrow experience and address the needs of others. Charity, volunteering, care for others – these make us feel we belong to a cause, movement or legacy, and put our other concerns into perspective. This is the meta-need that kicks in when we realize that we are not the only ones in the universe, and there is immense meaning and gratification to be found in serving something other than

ourselves. We may fill this need by contributing in actually harmful ways, however, when we force our vision on others, manipulate, gossip, boast or try to dominate.

Looking at this list, what stands out for you when you consider your own fundamental needs to be happy and whole?

Here are questions to help you determine which needs could use a little more attention. It may be a good idea to sit with a journal and consider each need taking your time and being honest.

How are you currently meeting each need?

Note that your approach may not necessarily be healthy or sustainable. You could be meeting your need for significance by being critical and judgmental of other people, for example, or your need for certainty by clinging to inaccurate core beliefs because "better the devil you know." Humans will do whatever they can to meet their needs – what are you doing to meet yours?

Are some needs going chronically unmet?

Look for any needs you are having trouble fulfilling. These may be those you try to satisfy using inappropriate means, for example, comfort eating to addressing a deep unmet need for love and connection.

How can you translate some of these unmet needs into goals for yourself?

Let's say you identify a need that is not being (properly) met in your life, for example, the need for variety. Maybe you are so bored with your job and your daily routine that you have resorted to a risky gambling habit just to feel something. Ask yourself – how can I satisfy my needs in a healthier way? Answering this question will help you set goals. In this example, you could set a goal to introduce other, healthier forms of stimulation into your life, like trying new things, doing extreme sports, travelling or taking up a challenging hobby.

Keep asking the above questions and you will inevitably learn more about what makes you tick – and what could make you tick better! The great thing about framing a self-coaching journey in terms of needs is that it naturally lends itself to taking concrete, beneficial action. Any time you are feeling bad, ask what need of yours is not being met. Then, in that very moment, ask what proactive steps you can take to meet that need more healthily.

Understanding Your Values

Though the self-help industry might sometimes have you believe otherwise, your identity isn't just something you go shopping for like you do a pair of sneakers or a brand of shampoo. You cannot just pick and choose values—they need to be a *genuine* expression of what you really do care about. This can seem a little like a catch-22 situation—you don't have an identity so you need to find your values, but how do you know which values you care about without having an identity?

The process is not as difficult as it seems.

Firstly, know that the process isn't done all at once—you are not going to uncover a complete and fully-functioning self in an afternoon and start living your best life once you wake up tomorrow morning. It's a *process*, and insight will come in fits and starts. In fact, a life well-loved might be one in which you continually revisit the question of identity, with your answers deepening on every attempt.

We also need to remember that, in finding values, we are the ultimate arbiters. We decide. So, you might need to take the time to tune out every other voice so you can better hear your own. There is no wrong way to do it. There's no right answer. There's only what works for *you*.

Having said that, people are motivated by a lot of different values, which it might help to consider in finding out our own:

- *Financial independence or wealth*

- *Being in nature*

- *Romantic love or connection with others*

- *Having freedom and independence*

- *Learning and knowledge*

- *Fun and adventure*

- *Good physical health and fitness*

- *Spiritual or religious pursuits*

- *Art and creativity*

- *Work accomplishments, leadership, business*

- *Security and survival*

- *Social cohesion and harmony in a group*

- *Peace, calm, and contentment; relaxation*

- *Honor, loyalty, and dependability*

... and so on.

You might look at all of the above and think that they're all valuable. But the trick is in identifying your *priorities*—those things that are best, that bring the most satisfaction and meaning. You may care about creative expression and individuality, but your love of family stability may trump that ten times over. You need to know how each of your needs and preferences rank relative to each another.

A good way to find out what matters most is to ask what has seemingly bought you the most happiness and sense of meaning in the past. If you look at all your high points in life, and they all involved adventure and freedom to travel and explore, that tells you something. It works the other way around too: in thinking of your life's most painful memories, why did they hurt so much? Could it be that these events were moments when your deepest values were disappointed or violated? Tally up the achievements you're genuinely proud of and see what they have in common. Or, look more closely at your worst failures and blunders and ask why they stung particularly badly—were these times where you acted *against* your values?

Another trick is to look at the people you admire or wish to be like (or even envy)—what values do they exemplify? If all your role models and heroes are self-made entrepreneurs, is this telling you about the value you place on financial independence? Maybe. Or maybe what appeals to you about them is that they're unique and following their own dreams, breaking the rules. Or maybe they are reflecting your yearning for a life filled with more admiration and recognition.

Since you are uncovering your values rather than creating them from scratch, another general technique is to look at all the decisions you are currently making—they may speak strongly to values you might not yet be aware you actually have. Watch yourself closely for a few days or a week, and notice your decisions when faced with a choice to make. Notice how you feel when you choose one thing over another.

It might be that you notice yourself often choosing things that leave you feeling bad, and don't really feel aligned with who you are. It may be that you notice key decisions reflecting your values. Either way, we are already living by values every moment of every day—it's simply a question of becoming aware of them and asking whether they're the choices that best reflect the values we hold—or want to hold.

Look for patterns. See if you can find any strong feelings one way or another—are there any non-negotiable sentiments? What are you absolutely unwilling to do or give up? Why? What choices make you feel proud and content, and which ones feel like a compromise, an obligation, or even something you're embarrassed about?

Feeling right, however, is just one aspect that helps determine your values. You also need to make informed decisions about what you really believe in that rely on more than just your emotional inclinations at any given time. Say you're confused about whether you value your career or your connection with friends and family more.

You've found that abandoning your family for work often leaves you feeling guilty, and so you think maybe you value your family more than your career. The next step here is to try to find out *why* you feel that way. There can be many factors external to yourself that are influencing this feeling of guilt. Maybe you just have FOMO (fear of missing out), or your family has ingrained a value system in you that says work should always come second.

To get a clearer picture of what valuing something really entails, it helps to read a little on the various reasons why one might want to prioritize something over the other. We are rarely aware of all the reasons one or the other might be a good idea. Just a few searches will yield several reasons for either choice. When reading these, don't just think about which reasons sound more appealing, think about what feels *right* to you. These will often have a lot to do with what your goals in life are. Are you really ready to sacrifice personal success to have a stronger bond with your family? Or would you rather focus on your career while ensuring your family is important, but not paramount?

Thinking in this way will prevent you from repeating the earlier cycle of simply having imbibed certain values from your surroundings without really considering what matters most to *you*.

Values (and the identity that comes with them) are not abstract. They are real, lived things, out there in the world. They express themselves in actions and choices. True, they may not always be expressed perfectly all the time. But the *intention* is to live by them. They are a yardstick by which to measure your life, whether you achieve that standard or not. This is why it's more effective to look at your actual life in action when considering values, rather than just sitting down with a piece of paper and pulling nice-sounding ideas out of your imagination. Remember, we are striving for the *real* self, and not just another false self.

What About My Goals?

Be honest with yourself. In asking what you value, you are halfway on the road to knowing who you are, and when you know who you are, you know how to act, and why. In trying to find your identity, you might be tempted to start thinking about your goals in life. But this is premature. You can only decide on your goals when you know what you value (and don't value!). How many of us have chosen a goal, only to reach it and realize it isn't what we really wanted, or it doesn't have the desired effect on us? It's probably because we didn't stop to think whether our goals actually lined up with our values.

Goals are important, but they emerge from our values—not the other way around. Yes, your interests and preferences matter. Your obligations and commitments matter. You need to make plans and understand your strengths and weaknesses. But all of this comes after you do the important work of setting up your values. Without them, you cannot undertake any other task with clarity, and you will have that nagging sense of aimlessness in your life—no matter how many impressive-sounding goals you come up with.

When we have our values clearly identified within us, it's as though life is suddenly clearly outlined, and we can see what is inside that outline and what is outside. We know what is relevant to us, and what is a distraction or a diversion. We know how to assess things, and how to measure our actions. We know where we're going and what we stand for. And all of this adds up to a life that feels *purposeful*. We don't feel wishy-washy or unsure of ourselves—instead, our identify firmly takes shape, and we are consciously aware of who we are and what we're doing. It's very simple: we cannot be fulfilled if we don't have values. Without values, we have nothing to compare our achievements against, and all our actions feel pointless. With values, however, life just flows so much more smoothly.

Consider an example. Someone might work hard to discover that their primary value in life is spiritual enrichment. Looking at their lives, they see how so much of their joy has come from reading spiritual and religious texts, volunteering, going to retreats, meditating, and taking plenty of time to be in nature, where they feel closest to the divine.

Because this value is strongly identified, it acts as a guiding force for everything in this person's life. When they're feeling depressed, they know to stop and ask, "Am I neglecting my spiritual needs? How can I reconnect to that feeling that sustains me and gives me hope?" When faced with a conflict with themselves or with others, they fall back on their code of ethics that comes from their values—they approach problems with compassion, forgiveness, and a little humor.

When they're standing in the checkout line at the supermarket and they see a trashy tabloid paper with a cover designed to inflame and aggravate, this person is able to stop, take a breath, and say, is this me? Is that who I want to be? Then they can turn away and choose not to engage with that kind of material in their life. What you eat and drink, what you say, where you live, the work you do, the clothes you wear—all of this reflects who you are and what you value. In this way, both big and small value decisions create a framework and a foundation for an entire life. When clarified this way, you can see how powerful it is to know one's own values.

Here's the thing: you already have values. Whether you got them from your family, your society, or Instagram, you have them. Whether you're aware of them or not, they're there, guiding your life. So why not make sure the values you have are something you consciously want?

We need to be careful that we are always tuning in to the *real self*, and not another *false self*. How many times have we heard about the person having a midlife crisis, or a teenager going through "a phase"? They seem to be trying on a few costumes in the attempt to settle on one that fits. People in these transitional states of life may cling to an identity they think they *should* have, or wished they did have, but it is still not a genuine reflection of who they are. This work takes patience, honesty, and a little determination (and yes, you may need to go through a few awkward "phases" yourself on the way!).

Now that we've seen what value-discovery *isn't* (it's not about goals, other people's opinions, or switching out one false self for another one), we can look more closely at what it is. Here's a step-by-step guide to bring you closer.

Value Clarification, Step by Step

STEP ONE: CLEAR YOUR MIND

If we wish to fill ourselves up with something new, we first need to pour out all the old that's already there, and start fresh. We need to let go of any bias, expectations, or preconceived notions. Being fixed in our thinking, we can imagine we already know the answer to everything—but this understandably undermines the process of discovery. You really need to trust that there is something for you to learn, something unknown out there that you are willing to encounter openly.

It's difficult, but try to drop (at least temporarily) any preconceived ideas about who you are. Your conscious mind may want to jump in and tell you a narrative ("you're an introvert, you're a worrier, you're XYZ"), but set these aside and give some space for your unconscious mind to come to the fore and see new possibilities. We have all been taught which values are "better" than others—we need to forget this lesson if we want to find our *own* values for ourselves!

STEP TWO: START A LIST

Remember that values aren't chosen, they're clarified. Trust that you already have them, you just have to *discover* them. You don't want to inadvertently write down a list of all the things that other people expect you to be.

Scan the list given earlier and see if any of them spark your interest. If not quite, how could you tweak them so they seem more valuable in your opinion? When compiling a list, start broadly and don't censor yourself. Add anything that strikes you as important. You might begin by writing "love," but on further reflection, tease that out a bit more. What kind of love, and why? You might decide that what you really value is brotherly love, friendships, belonging to a community. You could then put "community" on the list and see if that spurs any further values.

As you go, draw on both your best and worst life memories to guide you, as described above. The moments you felt most yourself—what was happening, and what were you doing? The moments when you felt frustrated, violated, disappointed, or uncomfortable—what was not happening, and what does this tell you about the feelings you hold dear?

You might recall the greatest day of your life so far, the birth of your first child. In thinking about why this felt so amazing, you jot a few more notes on your list. You realize that you felt a deep, deep sense of purpose knowing that you now had someone to look after. You examine those feelings of hope, of dedication, of amazement. You realize that being a parent satisfies some of your core values—selfless love, belonging, trust, and hope for the future.

Ask yourself questions to dig closer toward those things in life that bring a sense of meaning. What makes a good day good? What makes you proud and grateful? What makes life worth living (i.e. you'd be miserable without it)? Look not only at the standards you hold for yourself, but those you hold for others. What is a deal breaker for you in your relationships? What is your idea of a person *not* living a meaningful and purposeful life?

STEP THREE: PULL IT ALL TOGETHER

Eventually, you should have a long list of things you value. Though all of these things are important, they can probably be distilled down to a few *main* core values. Read over the notes you've made and see if you can group them into chunks. For example, "community," "friendship," and "compassion for others" have a lot in common, as do "independence," "freedom to follow my own path," and "part-time employment."

Remember, you are not judging anything you have on the list. If you genuinely identify it as a value, put it down. If, on further reflection, you really don't care all that much about innovation or winning awards, then leave them out. As you work (without attachment or judgment!), you should start seeing some clarity emerge. As much as you can, try to connect these ideas to real life—

are these values you've actually experienced before meaningful, or have you just been raised or socialized to assume that you want them?

Once you have some clusters of values, see if you can dig deep and identify the main theme uniting them all. In our examples above, friendship, compassion, and community all have one thing in common: the joy of shared human connection. Take your time with this—what is it, really, that makes all of the things on your list so appealing to you?

STEP FOUR: RANK YOUR VALUES

Some people might find that, even after clustering, they're still left with a big list. But, life is filled with choices, and since we are limited, we are often called on to choose between two important and worthwhile things. This is why we need to clarify further and prioritize our values.

You now want to whittle down to those essential values that you absolutely cannot live without. The most fundamental, most basic needs of yours, without which you'd be completely lost, miserable, or pointless. Even if you can identify a few of these, try to choose between five and ten values that you feel neatly capture the dimensions of what's most important to you.

Then, rank them in order of importance. You might do this in ten minutes or find you need a few days to really contemplate it deeply. Use your feelings as a guide, and remember not to rush—you are setting aside everything you know about your false self so that you can meet the acquaintance of your real self—that takes time!

STEP FIVE: LET YOUR VALUES COME ALIVE

If you write something like "physical health and fitness" as a core value, it may seem a little abstract. Time to embed this sentiment out in the real world and put it into context! You want to put these newly discovered core values into a shorthand form that will inspire you every time you look at it, and remind you precisely of the best things in life—according to your most authentic self.

For the person valuing physical fitness, a single beautiful image of a ballet dancer in a powerful leaping pose, mid-flight, might capture the essence of what you value so much: pushing against the limits of human physicality to find beauty and expression in the joy of having a living, moving body. Or, you might find that a certain phrase or quote captures your core value better, a bit like a mission statement. Find a stimulus that triggers a strong emotional reaction—it's these emotions that point you in the right direction and speak more directly to your inner self than any dry, abstract language could.

STEP SIX: TRY THEM ON FOR SIZE

No, you're not done quite yet! Value discovery is an ongoing process. Once you've identified and condensed your core values, see how they fit out in real life. Leave the list for a while and come back to it, seeing how it feels. Do you feel comfortable, in alignment, and clear . . . or are some things still not quite feeling like "you"? Look for the hidden voice of your parents, your culture, etc., and ask whether they've been swaying your list or the way you rank things. If your intuition pipes up, listen to what it says. This may sometimes feel like vague, flimsy work, but rest assured that you are exploring exciting new realms that many people never give themselves permission to enter.

And that's that. Your core values distilled into a concentrated essence that tells you a lot about who you are as a person, and helps you answer a range of questions from, "What should I do?" to, "What do I want right now?"

Visualizing Your Future Self

One final way to gain insight into who we are and what we want to achieve, is to turn our attention away completely from the present and instead immerse ourselves in what *could be*. What follows is a "best possible self" exercise, which helps you vividly visualize a potential future life for yourself.

You might immediately feel resistance to this – isn't it just pie-in-the-sky thinking? Shouldn't we focus on what can be concretely done in the here and now? The answer is yes. However, such an exercise is also valuable since it can shift our mood, reinvigorate old hopes and dreams we'd forgotten we had, and excite us about possibilities again.

Can you imagine a future in which you have achieved all the goals you set out to achieve, and things have turned out in the best way possible? The rules for the following visualization exercise are simple:

- Imagine a future for yourself that is perfect but also *attainable* (in other words, you want to brainstorm and let your imagination run wild, but there's no use imagining a future where you win the lottery 5 times in a row.)

- Imagine a time at some definite point in the future. You can choose a year, three years, five years or whatever you like.

- In this imagined future, think of who you would be spending time with, and what you would be doing. Think about how you would spend your moments, and what each day would look like. Especially imagine what you feel. What are the thoughts running through your head? What are your actions and what things do you say?

- Spend some time in each separate domain as you see fit – professional, personal, emotional, etc. See what it looks like in each area to have attained your goals.
- You can write down your thoughts or just spend some time, eyes closed, fleshing out an image in your mind's eye.

As you do this exercise, try to avoid getting carried away with the hows and whys. You're just imagining the end point, once all of that has been accomplished. Once you're finished with the exercise, you may feel more upbeat and optimistic. Simply allowing ourselves to dwell on possibilities has a surprising effect on our ability to start generating new goals. Tapping into this excitement and desire can be precisely the fuel needed to power work to bring that vision to life.

This technique works because of how your brain works. The more vividly you imagine something, the more your brain thinks it's "real." If you feel uncomfortable with this fantasy, remind yourself of two things:

- You are not imagining your wildest, most impossible dreams, but the very edge of what is attainable for you. Dreams genuinely within reach can be so much more energizing and empowering than pure fantasy.
- You are already practicing visualization anyway! Many of us are experts at catastrophic "what if" thinking, not realizing how this negative focus limits our perspective and impacts our decision-making. If you will visualize, at least do it consciously.

At first, you may find it difficult to flesh out a detailed picture in your mind's eye. Here, start with the most important element first: how it *feels* to achieve any goal. Focus on the warm feelings of accomplishment, peace, purpose, pride, joy, or gratitude, and then expand your awareness to all the events and situations that would most create this feeling for you. Often, it's difficult to see a way out of a problem or break old patterns of negative thinking because we literally picture nothing different. This exercise permits us to imagine a possible world in which the current challenge we are facing has been overcome. Ironically, this can sometimes be just what's needed to help us see a solution we didn't see before.

There are many ways to use this exercise to your benefit:

If you have two competing goals, you can "rehearse" the outcomes of each to gain clarity on what you most value.

You could start each day or week with this exercise to get you feeling optimistic and excited.

You could also use it as a buffer against stress: visualize before a challenging event or use it to help you unpack a difficult situation that's already happened. You can encourage yourself to visualize how expertly your future self manages conflict and comes out the other side.

The technique can be added to a regular journaling habit or used to start or finish a meditation or mindfulness practice. It's a way to breathe life and vitality into your goals, making them feel real, right now in the present.

If you feel anxious, this exercise is a way to counter catastrophic thinking and open your mind to positive potential outcomes rather than focusing solely on the negative.

When your motivation for a goal is flagging, remind yourself of why you're doing what you're doing by using this exercise. You'll get back in touch with what matters, and reaffirm your convictions.

Finally, this exercise is a way to "try on" different goals, life paths or options so you can try to preview the results you'll get. This can be powerful – you may discover that a goal you thought you cared about will likely not make you as happy as you imagined. By making the outcomes of your choices more visceral and emotional, you get to test-drive them and see if they're something you really want.

There is one big, big caveat, however. This exercise is not enough to change your life all on its own. Vaguely daydreaming about ways that things could be better is only useful if we take that experience and translate it into something concrete in the here and now. This is why it's so important to finish every visualization exercise in the same way: *tether it back to reality.*

Let's look at an example.

Imagine Annie sits down to do this exercise one afternoon. She has been feeling aimless in life, and not sure what she wants for herself. Annie is a professional video editor although she has long since grown disillusioned with what she once considered a "glamorous" job. A year ago, she was given more responsibility and a pay rise at work, but gradually she's wondering if her career is all that satisfying anymore. Still, though she suspects she should make changes to her career, she's not sure what that would even look like.

She decides to "try out" a few potential futures. She writes down three options in her journal:

1. Go part-time in the same job, downsize and pursue all the things I neglect because I'm busy at work
2. Do nothing and keep things as they are
3. Quit my job and re-train as a yoga teacher

She does a few minutes of meditation and then moves on to visualizing the first scenario. She pictures herself in the perfect life – she works only part of the day, and the rest of the day she's taking long walks, staying fit, reading fascinating novels, spending quality time with friends, and overall relishing life. She sees herself smiling broadly. She is relaxed, at peace, and confident in who she is. Her pace of life is slower, and she feels spiritually fulfilled with new opportunities to camp out in nature every week. She's even lost weight now that she's not stress-eating at work all the time.

As she explores this vision, she notices herself thinking and saying certain things to the people in her imagination. Things that surprise her. She says, "I've always been a rebel at heart" and "I feel best when I am free to follow what's important to me."

Later, she does the same visualization with the other two options, but neither of them generates the same excitement as the first. Though she originally thought that being a yoga teacher was a dream career for her, when she stepped inside that vision, she realized how much it would annoy her to have to stick to a schedule and cater to students. Instead, doing solo yoga when the mood struck her felt like what she wanted.

At the end of the 3 visualizations, Annie is convinced of one thing: she is sorely craving more independence and freedom. In her professional, personal, and emotional life, she decides she needs to create more room to be spontaneous and follow her own impulses. To keep herself grounded, she takes one small step towards her goal: she books a meeting with her boss to discuss more flexible working options.

Fast forward to six months later, and Annie has left her job. Her boss hated her idea of part-time work, so she quit and found another where she works only half the hours and has more flexibility. Now she's worried about money, she's moved to a new neighborhood with a lower cost of living, and she's apprehensive about the big lifestyle changes she's making. She returns to her old journal one day and finds the visualization exercise. She decides to repeat it.

In her next visualization, she pictures herself in three years. This time, her vision is much, much clearer. The ideas rush in easily. She sees herself thriving. Her life is filled with all sorts of activities and people, but one thing is for sure: it's not like anyone else's life. She can't quite see the details, but she can *feel* what it feels like to live a life that is independent and free.

She's barely done with the exercise before she starts excitedly making plans and goals. There's so much she wants to do: volunteer in the community. Take up dancing. Visit new places. And like a thunderbolt, she realizes with perfect clarity she *does* want to do yoga, but in a different way – *her* way. Wouldn't it be cool to create her own yoga videos? Then, she could create them at her leisure, using her existing video editing skills, and flesh out her own unique style. Without knowing that that was what she was doing, Annie has uncovered a truer, deeper calling in her professional life.

If Annie had only daydreamed idly taking no inspired action... she would still be daydreaming now. But she was able to take insights gained from the first exercise, act accordingly, and then feed her results back into the next time she visualized. She was using the exercise *proactively*, and it helped her clarify her goals and values, showed what she couldn't see before, and gave her an exciting new avenue to explore.

Visualization, then, is not just flimsy fantasy – it's a real way to generate novel perspectives, solve problems, clarify desires (and disqualify some), and help fine tune the path we're already on. Though all the exercises in this book may seem like they're discrete and straightforward, in life, we can mix and match, skip stages, return to old ideas, and blend theories as and when we need them. We can experiment, do trial and error, and keep anchoring against our original frame:

What do I want?
What do I currently have?
What could I do?
What will I do?

Visualization is a tool. It helps us put a finger on what we want, and can highlight all those things in our current reality we *don't* want. Its strength is its ability to connect us to the emotional component of our hopes and dreams. It can show us new possibilities and options, and give us the courage and enthusiasm to plan to act. If you're seeing the enormous potential of this approach, congratulations – you're thinking like a coach!

Summary

- To know the goals we should set, we need to know more about who we are and

what we value. Self-knowledge is a prerequisite for growth.
- There are many ways to learn more about yourself. One way is the Wheel of Life, which divides our being into 8 key areas. By carefully mapping out a pie chart showing how we rate each area on a scale of 1 to 10, we can see at a glance our relative satisfaction with each area. This can inform the goals we set for ourselves, for example by seeing where we are unbalanced or lacking.
- Another self-knowledge tool is to think of your life in terms of how well you are meeting the 6 basic human needs, most commonly understood to be love and connection, variety, significance, certainty, growth and contribution. There are healthy and unhealthy ways to meet these needs. We can create the most impactful goals by seeing which of our needs are not going met, or which are being met in an unhealthy way. We can ask: what is my need right now and what's the healthiest way to meet that need?
- Effective goal-setting can also come from knowledge of one's deepest personal

values and principles. Knowing what is most important to you – service, creativity, independence, etc. – will help you shape the goals that are most appropriate for your unique life.
- If you're not sure what your values are in life, don't worry; discovering them is not hard. However, the process does take time, and you won't simply wake up tomorrow with complete knowledge of what your values are.
- The first step to discovering what your values are is to simply abandon all preconceived notions you have of who you are. Often, the values we have been living by are actually derived externally. This can be through our family, culture, historical era, etc. By starting from a clean slate, we avoid such influences from clouding our judgment regarding our true values.
- Next, think about the things that you feel most strongly about. This could be personal success, close family bonds, serving others in the form of social work, etc. Finding one will often lead you to other values you hold because they point to a "higher" value you possess. Thus,

valuing family over career means that your interpersonal relationships in general are valuable to you.
- One final technique is to actively visualize your future self, living your best life, once all goals are accomplished. This can help you see new solutions, excite you about possibilities, and connect you to what you desire. Just remember to anchor any insights you have into reality by taking concrete steps towards those goals.

Chapter 3. The Power of Objectivity

Do we have a logical and useful framework to understand change? Check.
Do we have tools to help us identify who we are, so we know in what direction to change? Check.

Now, in this chapter, we'll explore a key capacity that will allow you to coach yourself – the ability to accurately and objectively perceive yourself. This skill is indispensable because, without it, we can never gain a neutral enough picture of how we're doing to know when we're doing it wrong! One benefit of a coach is that they're not you, and they don't have your hang ups and blind spots (you hope). So, they can call you out on your excuses, point out your resistance, or prompt you with a suggestion to help you get unstuck.

You can do this for yourself if you have enough objectivity.

First things first: self-observation and self-inquiry are not obvious, automatic or easy. Unless you deliberately commit to being objective, and unless you learn this skill from scratch, it's a mistake to assume you already are objectively aware of your reality. Often, we just assume we understand our weaknesses and strengths, that our perception of reality is accurate, or that we know when we're off-track and how to fix it. But how often do we check this assumption?

Let's begin with a straightforward way to generate more self-awareness: ask questions.

Self-Awareness Questions

The actual answers to these questions are not the important part. These questions are phrased as they are to challenge and inspire deep thought. They ask people to dive deeper into understanding *why* they answered the way they did, and dig into their behavioral and thought patterns.

1. What kind of prize would I work hardest for, or what punishment would I work hardest to avoid?

The answer to this question might help identify the true motive behind an individual's drive. Beyond surface-level things, what is really motivating people? Is this something they care about? And what type of pain or pleasure matters to them? On an instinctual level, what really matters the most in both a positive and negative way?

Gamblers all want one prize: the jackpot. They try and try again, whether it be scratchers or slot machines to try to win that big prize money. Is their hope that they will eventually win back all the money they've already spent into their gambling habit? Is their hope to become richer than they can imagine?

Why are they working so hard? You might discover that their motivation is the thrill and rush of the risk involved. Do they care about making steady pay or finding their purpose? Perhaps not. When you can dig into what someone wants the most and why, you can often find what is driving them without having to ask it directly.

When thinking of the prize you'd work hardest for, ask yourself how far you'd go to achieve that prize. This will often reveal the punishment you want to avoid most. A person might value money because to them, that is what success looks like. But what lengths would they go to for money? Would they break the law or cheat and deceive people? Maybe they're fine with being ambitious as long as it stays within some moral and legal bounds.

2. Where do you want to spend money, and where are you fine going cheap or skipping altogether?

This answer may reveal what matters to someone's daily living and what they want to experience or avoid in their lives. There comes a point when material belongings no longer have a meaning or purpose for someone. For example, sometimes, spending money on experiences instead of a new purse has the potential to improve someone's overall well-being and outlook on life.

What do you have no problem splurging on, and what doesn't matter to you? When deciding on vacation finances, people may opt to splurge on a boat trip and stay in a shabby hotel. This reveals their desire to experience an unforgettable moment rather than staying in a nice hotel, what they view as a waste of money. Others might opt for the opposite and revel in their creature comforts while not seeing much of the scenery. In either case, they've used their money to quite literally identify and spend their priorities. Ask yourself whether you prefer spending on experiences or materialistic possessions. Would you go on a tour to Europe, or buy the latest iPhone?

Where your money goes is an important part of what makes you happy, so if you can pay attention to where you let it flow and where you cut it off, you'll immediately know what matters to you on a daily basis.

3. What is your most personally significant and meaningful achievement and also your most meaningful disappointment or failure?

It is pretty common that experiences, whether they're good or bad, shape people into who they are for the present and future. Significant experiences also tend to create their self-identities—*you are this kind of person because you did this and succeeded or failed*. Achievements and failures tie into how someone sees oneself. Overall, it's about how people want to see themselves.

This question will get a response about how people view themselves, good or bad. Failure will evoke flaws they hate, while achievements will bring up strengths they are proud of.

A career woman who has worked her way up the corporate ladder might reflect on her accomplishments. She looks back to the things she did in order to get that corner office. She discovers that her resilience and determination helped her push through obstacles to get to where she is now. The story about her career accomplishments is actually a story about the positive traits she utilized in reaching that point—her self-identity. You can imagine the same negative type of self-identity might unfold if the same woman were to talk about her failures.

The way that people answer this question shows that they can identify positive and negative experiences and dissect why they hold particular values either so high or low.

4. What is effortless and what is always exhausting?

This question is designed to tell you where you should spend your time. Some people are better at things than others. Engineers are great at math, while artists are masters of creativity. Lawyers are great at arguing a point, while teachers do best at inspiring young minds. What might people say about you?

Whatever aspects of life, occupation notwithstanding, come easily and naturally to you are things you should emphasize and capitalize on. The things that are always challenging and exhausting may be worthwhile, but they may also be things you should simply let go of. The way people answer this question should help them tap into their best strengths and areas for improvement.

For instance, as a baker answers this question, she may automatically recognize her creative niche for blending ingredients together to make a beautiful dessert. She will see that although she has practiced perfecting her craft, it has naturally been very easy for as long as she can remember. She just sees outside the box in a way that few other bakers can.

On the other hand, it may take her much longer to write and follow traditional recipes. As she reflects on these natural strengths and weaknesses, she can look at herself and design a career that better suits her strengths and weaknesses instead of trying to conform to other people. This is all because she recognized her natural talents and followed them.

5. If you could design a character in a game, what traits would you emphasize and which would you ignore?

This helps people focus on their ideal selves. Imagine that you have a limited number of points to give a person but six traits to spread the points across. Which will you choose to emphasize and bolster, and which will you choose to leave average or even lacking? It's more than likely that this either represents how you see yourself or how you would like to see yourself. You might even create someone entirely different from who you are.

For someone answering this question, it helps them identify what they consider to be their strengths and flaws. The strengths you can continue to make front and center, while the weaknesses can be pinpointed to be worked on.

6. What charity would you donate millions to if you had to?

Besides reflecting on the needs of oneself, there now comes the test of someone's worldwide view. Asking this question forces one to think about the values and needs of others and what they care about outside of themselves.

Will you donate to an animal shelter or a charity for cancer? Perhaps you would sponsor a child from a third-world country? They all say very different things about you. Whatever the case, it tells you how you want to see the world and what types of causes matter to you.

Another version of this question is to ask what you would do if you won the lottery, or suddenly found that money was no object. Imagine you no longer had to work for money, and think of what you would fill your day with instead. Travel? Community work? Art? Education? Or would you have one big party with your friends and family?

Take the time to imagine your world with all the necessities of money removed, and you may be left with a clearer picture of who you are and what you value beyond practicalities.

How to Observe Yourself

"When you go out into the woods, and you look at trees, you see all these different trees. And some of them are bent, and some of them are straight, and some of them are evergreens, and some of them are whatever. And you look at the tree and you allow it. You see why it is the way it is. You sort of understand that it didn't get enough light, and so it turned that way. And you don't get all emotional about it. You just allow it. You appreciate the tree. The minute you get near humans, you lose all that. And you are constantly saying 'You are too this, or I'm too this.' That judgment mind comes in. And so, I practice turning people into trees. Which means appreciating them just the way they are." - Ram Dass

The biggest obstacle to clear, accurate perception is judgment. If you are making a judgment about something, then you are no longer perceiving – you are not in your sense organs, in the present, but somewhere far away in your mind, telling yourself a story that comes from a world of memories and fantasies and old ingrained patterns. When we judge, we make evaluations about things and decide if they're "good" or "bad." We encounter another person, or we have an experience, or we something in our reality (an emotion, an event, an idea) and we instantly think,

"This isn't supposed to be this way."
"That's a toxic thought."
"He's too forward."
"I'm such a loser."
"That's an overreaction."
"I'm less judgmental than they are."
"Oh, this one's the best!"

While this tendency may come from a need to control (remember the need for certainty and significance?) it closes us off from genuine experience, compassion for self and others, and the vitality of life. While *discernment* is a useful mental tool, our constant judgment doesn't keep us as safe or secure as we think it does. A judgmental attitude creates problems. It's a barrier that prevents connection and clouds accurate self-perception. And it doesn't feel all that great, either!

When you're on the path of self-development, it feels almost automatic to find fault with yourself, and to see all the ways you are not good enough, not there yet. The irony is that letting this tendency go is the thing that will allow you to genuinely appreciate and engage with your present enough to change it. Many of us wrongly believe that self-judgment *is* self-observation! Instead, we need to learn to **perceive without making any evaluations**. Here's how.

1. Gain distance

Detach yourself from what you're observing. Literally imagine yourself standing outside of it, unattached to it, unidentified with it. Give the phenomena enough space to be what it is. You can be bound up in an experience, or you can take a bird's eye view and look at it without you and your ego involved.

There are always two perspectives: you can be *inside*, unconsciously playing your role, or you can be *outside*, becoming aware of that role as a role. When you start to feel strongly about something, that's you going back into identification. But you can observe this, too. Say, "I can see my tendency to judge." When you do this, there is immediately something outside of that judgment, looking in. That's objectivity.

Try to look at what's in front of you like Ram Das looks at trees. It may help initially to reword your situation as though it were happening to someone else, or imagine that a stranger is telling the story of your situation. Instead of deciding whether it's good or bad, just open your mind and see *what is*.

2. Radically accept everything... even judgment

Here's a fun loop that mindfulness practitioners can get stuck in: they decide that judgment itself is "bad" and so go into judgment about their judgmental thoughts. Instead of being self-aware, they just become their own mind-policemen, monitoring themselves as though to pounce on any "bad" thoughts. Can you see how silly this is?

There's only one way out of the loop: do not judge even your judgment. If you notice you are having trouble with your lack of acceptance, what happens when you accept that nonacceptance? Judgment is just a habit we're taught by our past experiences and our environment. Certain thoughts and emotions can be lightning-fast and automatic. But if you are aware, in that moment, then you have a choice. You can go further into judgment, or you can see what happens when you just let things be what they are.

Radical acceptance doesn't mean you approve of what you observe. And it doesn't mean you condemn it either. It is possible to improve your life without having strong negative emotions about how your life is right now. Growing from a place of acceptance will always be more powerful than growing from a place of judgment and resistance.

The next time you see judgment, fear and insecurity rear its head, become curious. Without judging or labelling it, try to learn more. Where did this come from? What is its impact in your life?

3. Instead of black and white, appreciate grey

"The diversity of things, including bad things, help us know our personal preferences. How do we know what we do like if we don't know what we don't like? Diversity helps us identify what we desire. And knowing our desire is the first step in allowing what we want. Therefore, we don't judge. We observe things as they are, and see the positive impacts they bring in our process of creation." – Esther Hicks

Judgment narrows our vision. It breaks the world up into little pieces and pits those pieces against one another. But the world is as it is, and it doesn't need our permission, interpretation or judgment. In fact, life is so much richer, more diverse, more colorful and more vibrant when we stop insisting it obeys our limited ideas of "good" and "bad."

Inside our judgment boxes, we find more of the same. Stepping outside of those boxes, we find something new, something bigger than us. We find novelty, creativity, and solutions to problems. We find a bigger, transformative perspective.

One way to appreciate difference and diversity is to subtly change your language. Instead of saying things are wrong or bad, see what happens when you just call them "different." Shift away from emotive and judgmental language and just describe things as they are. "The weather's miserable" immediately shuts down any further perception. You could say, "It's raining a little right now. The clouds seem low, and I can see them kind of rushing along the horizon. There's a feeling of humidity on my skin, although there's not exactly a sense of heat. I can discern approximately nine different shades of blue and green in the sky overhead..."

4. Have compassion

So many people treat personal development like a torturous boot camp. They want to root out everything that's wrong with them and beat it out by force. When they observe themselves, they cannot help seeking out flaws, or making pronouncements and diagnoses. Having compassion for yourself doesn't mean you think you're brilliant and deserve praise for whatever you do (that would be a judgment). Rather, it's the conscious choice to treat your being – like every other being – as worthy of respect and acknowledgement for what they are.

Judgment means looking at reality and deciding one way or another that it should be something else. Acceptance and compassion mean simply looking at reality and acknowledging that it is reality. We can have compassion for our flaws. We can dislike a situation, or ourselves, and still have compassion because we are humans trying our best. We can see we are also like Ram Dass' trees – we are neither good nor bad. We just are what we are. Blame and shame only get in the way of us calmly and openly receiving whatever comes.

If we are hopeful and energetic, we perceive and accept that. If we are confused and angry, we accept that with the same openness. If we see we are changeable, we say "OK." If we make a mistake, OK. If we succeed, OK. In time, we realize that we deserve compassion, understanding, and acceptance regardless. Just because. Compassion is the respect we pay to things that are, because they are.

It can be a lifetime's work to clarify your own perception. Once you practice being objective, you may be surprised at just how often you are entangled in mental judgment, interpretation, and narrative that takes you out of the moment. But our consciousness is always there, and if we remove any obstacles in its way, we can see ourselves as we are. When we let go of the desire to constantly label things right or wrong, we are rewarded with something better: the ability to perceive what they actually are!

When we are unconscious and identified with phenomenon, no choice is possible. We only react. But if we are objective, we can change. To be proactive. We gift ourselves the possibility of doing something different.

Shining a Light on Your Blind Spots

Developing non-judgment and self-awareness is a worthy goal in itself, but in our mission to learn to coach ourselves, we can see it as a starting point. From the position of accurate self-awareness, we can see what we are doing, why, and how to do it better. Earlier in the book, we noted that the desire and capacity for growth is innate – but there sure are a lot of obstacles that get in the way. With self-inquiry and accurate self-perception, we can remove some of those obstacles.

When you're working with a coach of any kind, they will automatically provide you with feedback on how you're doing. They will ask you questions, bring certain things to your attention, or even outright challenge some of your assumptions. They will avoid judging you but instead highlight what you got wrong, why you got it wrong, and how to not get it wrong next time. To coach yourself, you need to have a similar mechanism in place. One way to do this is to turn that same nonjudgmental observation onto yourself. But don't do it all alone. If ever you're wondering about the accuracy of your perceptions of reality, look around you – the world is filled with other perceptions against which you can compare and contrast your own. Other people can be an invaluable resource if you know how to engage them in your growth.

It's a little like having someone to tell you when you have spinach on your teeth. All the self-awareness in the world can't show you what you're simply not aware of. But there is a knack for knowing how to elicit this useful information from other people. A 1996 paper published in the journal *Psychological Bulletin* showed that it may be much better to ask for advice than it is to ask for feedback. The researchers found that feedback intervention attempts were less successful the more they related to the person themselves, and not to the task at hand. Conventional feedback could even reduce overall performance.

Why? Well, think about the last time you were asked to give feedback. Most likely, you gave vague and generally kind responses that wouldn't hurt the other person's feelings. But when the researchers designed an experiment to look at the difference between feedback given to a *person* vs. appraising feedback for the *task* they'd completed, they found differences: people were much more critical and detailed when asked to evaluate a task and not a person. They also found that people asked to give "advice" gave more actionable responses than when asked to give "feedback."

"Feedback" is associated with evaluations leveled at individuals – something most people are reluctant to give, even when anonymous. However, "advice" is more neutral, and less about the person doing the task than the task itself. It's the difference between saying, "this presenter sucks" and "this presentation needs a stronger conclusion at the end." If your goal was to genuinely improve your presentation, then you'd want the second kind of advice, rather than the first. This is because the second contains a way to improve. The first just make you feel bad.

When you ask someone for feedback, you are asking them to go in evaluative mode. They may (correctly) sense you are looking for validation or praise, and subtly say what they think you want to hear. But if you ask for advice, you are telling them you genuinely want to get better. You are telling them that your focus is on the task, and not yourself. You invite them to look at your performance, and not *you*. They will tell you what they know. Then you're getting somewhere.

Whether we call it advice or feedback, we need to be careful of the information we elicit from others. Not everyone will be able to supply us with actionable, accurate information about our performance. What people have to say about you may just be a reflection of their own blind spots, and not helpful. You probably already know that unconstructive criticism can do more harm than good.

Receiving information from others can help us see our blind spots, give us a fresh perspective and prompt us to our next insight. But it needs to be done right. Your goal is to see how your vision aligns with other people's. The bigger goal is to see how well it aligns with "reality." You want to rid yourself of your blind spots and learn of your weaknesses.

Psychologist Tasha Eurich has discovered through her research that people are seldom as self-aware as they think they are. Endless introspection and navel-gazing by themselves don't lead to an increase in self-awareness – we need to pair our internal awareness (i.e., develop an accurate perception of who we are and what we want) with external awareness (i.e., accurate perception of how others see us).

External self-awareness is the ability to see how your behavior affects others, and how others see you. And this isn't something you can discover by sitting and writing in your journal! Instead, getting valuable and actionable feedback about your blind spots is something of art itself. Here's how to get the most from it:

Step 1: Identify who you can ask

In her book *Insight*, Tasha Eurich writes, "feedback from one person is a perspective; feedback from two people is a pattern; but feedback from three or more people is likely to be as close to fact as you can get." And that's something to remember: you are not eliciting random opinions from just anyone. You are trying to get as close to the "reality" of the situation as possible. This means you are after *facts*, and not value judgments about your character (remember the difference between advice and feedback).

Who should you ask for feedback or advice? Choose those people who you can trust to know what they're talking about. See how they appraise other things in the environment. Do you value their judgment generally? Choose people who will understand what is being asked of them, i.e., they will know that you need objective information about your performance and perspective, rather than for them to merely pronounce "good" or "bad."

Be careful with this – you may be tempted to ask someone you already know is a big fan of yours, because unconsciously you both realize that their "feedback" will essentially be praise and validation. Sometimes the people closest to us are the least objective about our performance, because they are too focused on *us* and not the *task* (this is why praise from your mom is so lovely but so useless!). There's nothing wrong with praise if it's what you need, but it won't help you improve upon your weaknesses. To improve, ask experts you trust, mentors, people who have achieved the goals you want to achieve, and those who themselves seek advice – this shows they understand and value the process. Finally, don't just get one view – get as many as you can.

Step 2: Prepare how you will ask
As we've seen, you should preferably ask for advice and not feedback. Prime the other person to give you useful information by telling them that your aim is not to stroke your ego, but to genuinely uncover blind spots and improve. Then, tell them what you are struggling with, and how you're framing your problem. Tell them why you are asking them specifically for feedback or advice, and emphasize that you are looking for their perspective on the task at hand, rather than your value as a person. You can frame your request for information with some well-chosen questions, for example:

In your opinion, what I am doing right now that is working?
What do you think I'm not seeing in this situation right now?
If you were in my shoes, how would you behave?
What advice do you have for me?
What single thing do you believe I could do to improve my approach right now?
How would you characterize the problem I'm experiencing?

Step 3: Be prepared to value what you are told

Truth be told, many of us seek advice and feedback without the slightest intention of listening to it. Unconsciously, we are just looking to be told that we are right to do what we are already doing. But this is the mindset of someone who cannot grow. To improve, you need to entertain that you don't have things figured out just yet. This takes honesty and humility.

When people give you the feedback you ask for, take a moment to listen. Be genuinely prepared to hear something you haven't thought of (that's the point, right?). Don't assume you're being attacked – if you ask people to be honest, you'll irreparably damage trust if you then punish them for being honest! Get your ego out of the picture, i.e., don't jump in to argue, defend yourself or explain. You too can switch your focus to the task rather than to who you are as a person, i.e., don't take it personally.

Even if you feel a little surprised or hurt, or you disagree with the feedback, say thank you (and mean it) and move on. You will have time to process what you've been told later – just accept the gift of feedback you've been given. You will demonstrate to others that you value their input, making it more likely they can be a source of support for you in the future, and you will show yourself the same respect. Growth and change aren't easy – if we can embrace the tricky and uncomfortable parts, we are standing with ourselves as we figure things out.

In time, receiving feedback won't seem like such a big scary thing. You may learn to relish it, because it helps you improve in ways you could never achieve on your own.

You can recognize and value those special relationships where the other person genuinely wants to be a part of our development, and knows how to guide and advise you.

Step 4: Do something about it
Now, it's time to remember that people are just people, opinions are just opinions. You can entertain feedback you've given without agreeing with it or taking it on board. But if you do it, do it because it's not useful, and not because of resistance or a dent in your ego.

If you've solicited feedback from a handful of people whose opinions you value, and they all say the same thing, then honor what you've been told by doing something about it. Take action. There's no point in seeking a perspective shift or new insights if they are not translated into concrete changes in your life.

Let's return to the GROW model – the feedback we receive can go towards our understanding of Reality. It can help us see new Options. And it can help us adjust or alter our goals. Often, if advice is good, it will feel like something we unconsciously sort of knew already. Even if it points to something a little unflattering, we see the truth in it. Sometimes, all we need is to have this reflected to us from the outside to have the courage to face up to it on the inside.

Once you've used your feedback to inspire concrete actions and set new goals, tell the people you've asked that their perspective has been useful, and what you intend to do with it. This may show more gratitude for what they've done than merely saying thank you.

The above process would work well in a professional context, or if you were training in some discipline or area where others might be expected to mentor you. It's also useful to receive useful insight on a specific performance or creation, and you want to know how you've done. But what if you want to improve your external self-awareness in a more general way? What if you're more interested in how you appear to others in personal relationships?

The Johari Window Technique

Here's an exercise you can do to help you better understand your relationship with yourself, and your relationship with others. The Johari window is a matrix of four quadrants made from two interacting factors: known to self or not known to self; and known to others and not known to others. There are four combinations of each of these:

	Known to self	Not known to self
Known to others	Open area	Blind spot
Not known to others	Hidden area	Unknown

Johari Window Model

Things are known to both self and others: This quadrant is called **open** or **arena**.

Things that are not known to self, but known to others: This quadrant is called **blind**, and shows us what others can perceive about us which we are actually unaware.

Things that are known to the self, but not known to others: This quadrant is called the **façade**, and it's the "hidden self" or even perhaps just the things you believe are true about yourself, but aren't objectively perceived.

Things that are not known to self or the other are called... **unknown**. Nobody perceives them, including the self. That's because they're not there, or because they are but remain hidden from view.

Now, let's imagine that people can be described by a list of traits or adjectives such a "shy" or "adaptable." One way to discover the accuracy of such labels is to compare perspectives. To make use of this technique, begin with a set of such adjectives – you can make your own or find a collection online. Now, with another person or in a group, first, take the time to choose all the adjectives you feel best describe you, positive and negative. You can also list adjectives you feel belong to the other person/people.

The magic comes in when you compare the lists. Construct a Johari window with four quadrants, and fill it in. The last square, the unknown, will necessarily be empty. But if you and the other people agree on an adjective, it goes into **arena**. If they chose an adjective you haven't chosen for yourself, it goes into **blind**. If you choose an adjective that they don't, it goes into **façade**. Everyone's windows can be completed this way.

You may be very surprised at your results. The most interesting quadrant is usually the blind one, and it functions much like consensus feedback or advice you never considered before. The difference between seeking feedback and doing this exercise is this really *is* personal – you are seeking mismatches between the perception of your self by others, versus your self-perception. It's not about the task but your identity. This is why this exercise is usually performed in therapeutic or life-coaching sessions rather than at work (can you imagine the drama?).

We can use the Johari window to generate intelligent and useful goals. For example, if you discover a massive difference between your self-concept and how you are perceived by others, you can try to better communicate, "show up" more authentically, or reconsider the image you're portraying. Likewise, if we merely believe ourselves to be, for example, "complex" whereas everyone else perceives us as "self-absorbed" that tells us something. Should we do a better job of accurately transmitting our complexity, or are we fooling ourselves that there is complexity in the first place?

Questions for Each Stage of Your Journey

When you lack objectivity and self-knowledge, you live a life in reaction to events you see as beyond your control. But with a clear framework for change, with the understanding of who you are and what you want, and with the ability to step outside of your life and see it for what it is, your life is no longer in control of you – you are in control.

As we gain more objectivity, we can consider more and more things as tools, rather than non-negotiable facts of life we can do nothing about. We see that our choices can be different, our thoughts and feelings can be different, and even the way we structure our identities and worldviews can be different.

The way we explore these possibilities is through curiosity and questioning. When we ask ourselves questions, we are allowing our curiosity and sense of possibility to lead the way, rather than lazy force of habit or fear. When we ask ourselves questions, we are deliberately putting ourselves in a generative, open frame of mind. To ask a question is a humble act, since it assumes we don't already know the answer. Truly, asking the right questions is halfway to getting the right answers.

With a conventional coach, questions can shape and guide your progress. When you coach *yourself*, you have to learn to use questions to sniff out your own way, uncovering insights as you go. And the questions that work with one problem or at one point in your life may not work at other times. Evolution doesn't happen overnight – it happens incrementally. It takes time. Especially if the transformations we're seeking are big ones, we need to gradually move through stages of understanding, one step at a time. Here are ideas for questions for each stage of the journey.

Clarity Questions

At the start of your journey, the path ahead may not be clear. You may begin with nothing more than a vague sense of unhappiness, but have no goals or any sense of how to improve your situation. This lack of clarity usually comes with a lack of self-knowledge, which the exercises earlier in this chapter have hopefully helped in revealing. But that's not a problem! You are at the exciting stage of your development where your challenge is to gain clear understanding of the *direction* you want to go in. Picture your excitement and energy as a compass pointing you in the right direction.

Get out your journal and work your way through these questions, and notice any recurrent themes in your responses. There are no right or wrong answers but do answer honestly and pay attention to what you feel most resistance towards. You guessed it – insight is waiting for you if you can become curious and ask about that resistance!

What are the 5 things that are most exciting to you in your life right now?
When have you felt happiest and most fulfilled in the past? Why?
What kind of work do you "lose yourself" in?
In your obituary, what would you most like others to say about you?
Who are the people you most admire in life and why?
What accomplishment are you most proud of achieving so far in life? Why exactly does it make you proud?
What is the one word your closest friends would use to describe you?

This may feel very broad but in time you can narrow down these themes, values, and overarching life purpose into specific goals. One final question brings all of this to a point: can you see any recurrent patterns in your answers? Return to the questions, *what do you want* and *who are you*? What do your answers tell you about what matters, and what doesn't matter?

Purpose Questions

Once you know what is important to you, then it's easier to explore your purpose. Think of it like discovering a strange new tool in an abandoned shed: if you know what the tool *does*, you know what it *is*. These questions can help you dig deeper into what your purpose in life is – not just your next goal, but your overall intention in all of life, and everything you do.

If today was a perfect day, what would it look like (this is like visualizing your future self)?
What did you want to do when you were a young kid, and what was your first interest and inclination?
On your death bed, what will you imagine you'll look back on and be most satisfied with if you could achieve it?
If money was no object and you had all the time in the world, what would you do?
When was the time you felt most hopeless, uninspired and lost? What is the opposite of the situation you were in then?

Challenge Questions

Once you are tapping into your truest life purpose, you will naturally want to make goals in that direction and do what you can to achieve them. And the second you do that, you will encounter obstacles. Yes, even if you're following your life's purpose! Perhaps even especially if you're following it.

After exploring who you are and what matters to you, and after figuring out your purpose, at some point, you embark on a journey to make the possible real. You set up a business. You seek a life partner. You sign up for that course or create your masterpiece. You step foot in the gym for the first time in 15 years. You sign up to volunteer at the community center.

And then things go wrong. Temptation, boredom, fear, doubt, setbacks, or outright failure. Just because you are heading in the right direction and ultra-passionate about your goals, it doesn't mean things are easy! You still need to stay curious, and keep asking questions:

What exactly is standing in your way right now?
What is under your control and what is not under your control?
Are you self-sabotaging? Why?
Can you foresee any challenges likely to emerge in the future? What could you do now to avoid them?
What is your biggest weakness right now?
What would it take for you to break through this current challenge?
What resources do you have to help you through this challenge?

Action Questions

As we know, nothing means anything until it's made concrete out in the world through action. Action is like a bridge that carries your intentions and dreams from the realm of the possible into the realm of the real. To prevent us from getting bogged down in endless self-reflection and loops of inward inquiry, we need to think like engineers and engage with reality to design, shaping, and influencing it:

What am I doing right now, and what results am I getting?

What is not working for me right now?

If there was only one thing you could do this year to not feel regretful, what would it be?

How can you convert your insights into concrete actions, not in the future but right here, right now?

What are the actions you hope to be taking in 3, 5 or 10 years from now? What should you do today to bring you closer to that?

Were you advising someone else in your situation, what's the one thing you'd tell them to do?

If you don't take action right now, what will be the cost? Both today and in the distant future?

What is the one thing stopping you from taking steps towards your goal?

When we coach ourselves, we use something a little like the scientific method – we ask questions, we devise hypotheses and experiments to test them, take risks and make changes, observe the results we get, become curious about why things happen as they do… and then we try all over again.

Getting-unstuck Questions

Along your journey of self-development and growth, you will sometimes shoot forward with enormous energy and clarity. Other times you'll bumble along slow and steady, and occasionally you'll stop completely, stumped by a hurdle in the path. At times like this, you must make a quantum leap in thought, to transform not *what* you are thinking but *how* you are thinking. There's no getting around it: you need to get unstuck to move forward.

Near the end of your journey, you may find you need to check back in with your original intention, change the plan, or completely change direction. You'll know you're stuck if you suddenly feel a little lost or unmotivated, confused or avoidant. Ask yourself:

What goal are you trying to achieve? Have you lost your way?
If you can do only one important thing today, what would it be?
Have you ever felt this way before? Did it last forever? What helped you get un-stuck then?

What could you do right now that you know would make you feel better in the next 24 hours? A week? A month?
What are your ultimate values and principles? What would your ideal self do in a situation like this?
What have you accomplished so far?
If you were being completely honest with yourself, what would be the thing you need to admit to yourself?

The great thing about these questions is that they all encourage a degree of objectivity – instead of being mired in a situation, you are standing outside of it, turning it over to see its different dimensions and aspects. Merely understanding that development is a journey is an insight because it invites you to be patient, and to tailor your approach to the stage you're at. One final exercise of objectivity is to literally imagine an alter ego that is a coach – or even better, a wise elder, expert or even deity that knows all. Imagine them looking at you in your situation and asking, what does this person need at this point in the story?

Summary

- Objectivity is an essential skill on the path to being your own coach, since it allows you to step out of your perceptions and see them from a distance, rather than getting identified and entangled with them. The best way to gain more self-awareness is to be curious and ask questions – in the first place, we should be aware of our subjectivity and realize that our perception differs from reality.
- The best way to gain self-awareness is to ask about your behaviors and actions, not your intentions or thoughts. Your thoughts are too easily corrupted or otherwise simply not representative of what you actually feel. When you can analyze your behaviors and actions, you can then glean real information about yourself.
- There are several questions you can ask yourself. For example, what is one achievement that you're most proud of and one thing you've done that you're most ashamed of? The achievement you're proud of will reveal a lot about what you value, and what kind of skills

you are good at that made the achievement possible in the first place. On the other hand, the thing you're ashamed of is something you should be wary about repeating and reminding yourself that you do not want to be the same person who did that horrible thing.
- Judgment hinders clear and objective perception. We judge from a position of fear or a need for control or certainty, but it's a skill to perceive things as they are, without assigning values, narratives or interpretations.
- We can gain more objectivity by comparing our perception against other people's when we ask for advice (which is better than asking for feedback, since it centers on the task and not you personally). We need to pick people whose perception we trust, and ask the right questions, and be prepared to take on what they say without ego and defensiveness.
- The Johari window technique is a great way to compare how we see ourselves with how others see us. We want to learn what others can see in us which we can't.

- The right question depends on the stage of the journey you're on. Initially, you can ask clarity questions to refine goals, then purpose questions to figure out your values and real desires. Challenge questions help you clarify your approach to setbacks and difficulties, while "getting unstuck" questions are there to get you moving again when you're lacking motivation, clarity or insight.

Chapter 4. Attitude is Destiny

Speaking of questions, here's a brilliant one: for what are you willing to struggle?

What kind of pain would you like to have in your life? To what end?

When we set goals and imagine futures, we focus on the good feelings, the reward, the sense of meaning and contentment. We ask ourselves, "what do I care most about?" or "what do I most want?" But merely wanting something is not enough to actually achieve that. There *will* be struggle along the way. There *will* be pain. The question is, what kind of life are you willing to pursue despite this pain and struggle?

We all want financial success, but not all of us are willing to accept the pain and struggle that comes with working our butts off.

We all want to be fit and gorgeous, but not all of us are willing to accept the pain and struggle that comes with working out all the time.

We all want to develop useful skills or create something of value, but not all of us are willing to put in the learning and practice required.

The biggest difference between the people that achieve their goals and the people that don't is that the successful ones were willing to suffer for what they wanted. It's not only about what good you like most, but what bad you are most able to tolerate. Not every motivational teacher will say so, but if a goal is worth anything, it will be hard work to achieve. Our success is not dependent so much on how vividly we can picture the happy result, but on how steadfastly we can endure the discomfort along the way.

If someone says, "I want to lose weight, and I commit to that goal", are they saying yes to the after picture where they're already thin and toned and happy? Or are they committing to the hard work, day in and day out, of daily exercise and good eating habits? They are probably not enthusiastically agreeing to all the times they must turn down delicious food that they'd rather enjoy. And yet, without the ability to do just that, they will fail.

In this final chapter, we're looking closely at the obstacles most likely to derail any genuine attempt at change: ourselves. A poor attitude is the biggest threat to you achieving your goals. Luckily, we have a good idea of the attitude most correlated with actually getting stuff done. And it might not be what you think: the change mindset isn't flashy or glamorous, not ultra-confident or enthusiastic, not brave and invulnerable. Instead, change happens most reliably when we are resilient to discomfort, patient, and humble. Let's look closely at these "best practices for change":

Embrace the Pain of Self-Discipline

Ultimately, what we may be looking for when we think about self-coaching and self-growth is hardening ourselves and gaining the ability to simply push through tasks more often than not. That's the very definition of self-discipline.

The brain can be tricked, mindsets can be shifted, and we can manipulate our surroundings all we want. At the core, we still need to engage in something we find at least slightly annoying or uncomfortable. Evidence is everywhere. For instance…

"Lose weight without the diet and exercise!"

"Think positively and you'll get whatever you want, without effort!"

"Follow this plan and you'll only have to work four hours in a week!"

In our modern consumer world, where marketing and advertising compete for our attention and our money at every turn, the name of the game is offering something for nothing. Abs without crunches. Money in the bank without breaking a sweat. Knowledge without studying too hard.

Products like this are successful because they tap into humankind's collective desire to avoid discomfort at all costs. We all have the dream of living in a world where we get everything we want without trying too hard or being scared or making any sacrifice. Otherwise, what's the lottery for?

However, as we've seen, a massive part of success in life comes down to self-discipline, and self-discipline is at its core made of nothing but the willingness to endure discomfort. In other words, there are no shortcuts, no easy life hacks, no quick tricks. Success in the bigger picture belongs to those who have mastered the ability to tolerate a degree of distress and uncertainty and who can thrive in situations of sacrifice in service of something bigger than their immediate pleasure in the moment.

Self-discipline = being uncomfortable. No tips or tactics needed.

We all want to grow and achieve, but the truth is that the state of growth is inherently an uncomfortable one. Evolving feels uncertain and risky at times, and it certainly requires us to give up immediate pleasures and old, easy habits. Growth and development is about expanding, risking, exploring. It cannot be done without leaving the security of the old behind. And sometimes, change requires pain, as the old dies and the new is still small and uncertain.

Self-discipline is not required for the easy parts of life. It takes no effort or special technique to enjoy what we already enjoy. But if we want to productively approach the rest of life, we need to develop the self-discipline to work with the things we don't enjoy. Rather than thinking of pain, discomfort, and uncertainty as roadblocks in our way to pleasure and success, we understand that they're simply a part of life, and if we manage them well, we can unlock even bigger pleasures.

There is a great paradox in learning to not just tolerate but embrace discomfort. Practicing being uncomfortable doesn't sound like much fun, and it isn't. But it is a skill that will reap far more rewards in the long term than merely chasing fleeting pleasures or shifting fancies in each moment.

Simply, we practice self-discipline and familiarity with discomfort because we respect that life contains an inevitable amount of discomfort. We know that in gaining a new perspective on the things we don't really want to do, we actually create new opportunities for fulfillment, meaning, and pleasure. Life becomes easier, and we become stronger, almost larger than the everyday trials and troubles life can throw our way.

With self-discipline, our expectations become healthier and more in line with reality. Our work becomes more focused and purposeful and we are able to achieve more. Self-discipline is not a thing we simply decide we want or think is a good idea in theory. It's a practice that we pitch up for again and again, every day and every moment, willing to work it out in the arena of our lived experience. In other words, self-discipline is a habit in a world where the easiest thing is to take the path of least resistance or fall prey to the "succeed without trying" traps all around us.

It might seem logical at first to pursue pleasure. But if there's one thing we know with utmost certainty, it's that things *will* change around us, we *will* have to endure suffering at one point or another, and we *will* be uncomfortable and forced to face things we wish we didn't have to. If we have this knowledge, isn't it better to be prepared rather than blindly pursue a dazzling goal with no thought to what you'll do when that goal doesn't go how you planned?

Learning how to tolerate distress, uncertainty, doubt, and risk while things are okay (i.e., before these things are forced on you by life) gives you the opportunity to practice and develop your discipline so you're prepared for future discomfort. Yes, it means that walking barefoot makes you more "immune" to one day having to walk without shoes. But it also means you're less attached to needing shoes, and you feel deep down that you are more than able to respond to and endure challenges. This is an attitude of empowerment. It's looking at life's challenges head-on and deciding to accept them and respond with dignity and grit.

Practicing tolerance is a "vaccine" in that you inoculate yourself against future discomfort in general. Adversity will still bother you, but you'll move through it with the quiet confidence that it won't kill you. How can it, when you've endured it all before and only came out stronger?

You can turn your focus to maximizing pleasure and refusing to engage with pain; or you can acknowledge that life intends to serve you heaping doses of both, and if you can prepare with maturity and wisdom, you can stay calm and ride those waves, trusting that you've developed your ability to survive.

So prepare while the going is still easy. Don't wait for life to force you to learn the lessons you must, sooner or later. Take the initiative by developing self-discipline right now. The shift is only a small one, but mentally it has great influence on how you approach yourself and life. The idea is straightforward: get more uncomfortable than you'd usually be. Give yourself the gift of the opportunity to grow stronger.

Importantly, you're not just thinking about these things or talking about them. It's not enough to "get" the concept intellectually or abstractly. One must actually have a *real lived experience* of discomfort. You need to get your hands dirty out there in the trenches of real life.

Develop self-discipline either by putting yourself in uncomfortable positions or by deliberately choosing to forgo comfortable ones. Train your will and discipline in the same way you would any other muscle: with repeated exercise. Become the person that is able to push through and do what others dread doing; become the person who can resist doing what everyone else can't resist. The way to do that? With a finely cultivated ability to tolerate discomfort and forego pleasure.

No, you are not being a masochist. You are not a glutton for punishment who wants to martyr themselves on the personal development altar and make a big show of how poorly they can treat themselves. It is actually your desire for a better, more meaningful life that moves you; it's because you ultimately want to make things easier that you are willing to have them be harder for a while.

Again, the paradox is that deliberately engaging with discomfort sometimes shows you just how insignificant it sometimes is. It allows you to enjoy the pleasures on a richer, deeper level. It's like forcing yourself to look under the bed to check for monsters. In the same way that there never is a monster, self-discipline can also teach you that doing without what you think you "need" is sometimes far easier than we think and that we're far stronger than we believed. Without giving yourself the chance to confront distress head-on, you might always cling to ideas of what you could never endure (i.e., certain the monster is still under the bed because you never gathered the courage to check).

Cold showers, going underdressed for the cold, sleeping on the floor, or foregoing food for a while don't sound like fun, but they are certainly something you can bear. They're all something that you can go through and come out the other end—intact! Afterward, take notice of how you feel. You may be surprised to note a feeling of calm confidence and achievement. Rather than being diminished by the experience, you might feel enriched, in a small way.

You can remind yourself as you endure the discomfort that, with each moment, you are making it more and more likely that you will better cope with adversity in the future. This knowledge gives you confidence and also reduces your fear of the unknown. When you can anticipate a negative outcome and be prepared for it, the future doesn't seem so threatening, and risks seem easier to manage.

You don't want to do any of it, sure. But you can. That's a skill. You *can* take cold showers. You *can* sleep on the floor. You *can* go without food. You *can* bear discomforts when they come. You can proactively manage your own fear and insecurity and get on top of it, rather than have it control you. And better yet, you are better equipped to respond in a world filled with quick fixes, distractions, and easy pleasure.

How does one actually practice all this, though? What does it look like in day-to-day life to cultivate self-discipline?

As a first step, don't dive into the deep end. Build up your confidence and your tolerance bit by bit. Perhaps you decide you'd like to stop mindless distractions like browsing online or looking at your phone constantly. Rather than throwing your phone in a lake and vowing to go offline completely, you instead ratchet up the discomfort slowly, giving yourself time to acknowledge and absorb the feeling of being able to manage. First, you decide not to keep your phone next to your bed. You notice the urge to have it anyway and notice feelings of boredom and the urge to grab it and get that easy dopamine hit.

You tell yourself, "I can do this. I'm in control. It's okay to feel uncomfortable. I'm staying with this feeling of discomfort."

And, lo and behold, you discover you can endure it. You make a habit of it. No arguing, justification, excuses, or avoidance. You simply acknowledge, "Yes, it's uncomfortable. Yes, I don't like it. But that's okay. I can do this."

Next, you inch up the discomfort. You've done the hard work of starting and you've given yourself proof that you can indeed bear discomfort. Now, you can push it a little. Perhaps you decide to whittle your mindless phone scrolling to just an hour a day. It's a small goal, but you achieve it. You feel proud of having done it. You may even notice that this pride feels better than the fleeting moment of entertainment or distraction you got from scrolling in the first place. You keep telling yourself, "I can do this."

Keep going. Gradually push yourself out of your comfort zone. Notice when you're pushing back against your decision. Sit quietly with your discomfort, whatever it looks like. It might take the form of anger or irritation. It might suddenly become very clever and try to convince you how unnecessary this all is and how you might as well cave because it doesn't matter. It might get depressed at having to engage with an emotion it feels entitled to be free of.

Simply watch all this come, and watch it go. Feel the calm you have in the wake of successfully enduring all this discomfort.

Isn't it wonderful to know that you can stand calm and strong through the storm? Tell yourself, "It's okay that I'm feeling discomfort. I'm in control. It will pass."

Finally, you might start to notice interesting things happen the more you practice. Watch your discomfort and watch your growing and changing response to it. Are certain things getting easier? Are you becoming familiar with all your idiosyncratic ways of resisting discomfort internally? Say to yourself, "I am capable of sitting with discomfort and any other negative feelings that may pass. I'm watching with curiosity. I will stay here with myself and with the feeling. I can do this. I will not respond with avoidance or escape or resistance. I welcome the experience. I can do this."

Of course, the other side of learning to tolerate discomfort is not just to endure negative feelings but to deliberately put off positive ones. Self-denial is the other side of the same self-discipline coin. Many addictive behaviors have their root in our inability to forego easy pleasure in the moment and bear the reality of the moment just as it is, right now.

Flex your self-discipline muscle by learning to say no to some of your impulses and urges. Train yourself to understand that you can act, even if you don't feel like it, and you can turn down an action, even if you really feel like doing it. As above, give yourself the opportunity to notice the feeling of calm strength this gives you.

Skip eating that sweet treat you go for automatically. Turn off the TV after one episode and force yourself to stand up rather than get sucked into three more episodes. Bite your tongue rather than say something regrettable to someone. A little self-denial opens up a crucial window of opportunity in which you can pause and deliberate on your actions. Are they in line with your ultimate goals? Do you *really* need to do them? What would you gain by turning them down for once?

Self-restraint and presence of mind enhance your sense of empowerment and control. Rather than being reactive and unconscious in your habits, stop and sink into the feeling of not fulfilling every desire, not acting, not going the easy way, or abstaining. It's a counterintuitive approach, but one that only yields greater and greater rewards the more it's practiced.

Here is a brief passage from *Meditations* by the Roman emperor-philosopher Marcus Aurelius that illustrates what we lose by surrendering to discomfort (of which is no concern to him) and not taking steps toward what we want in life:

> At dawn, when you have trouble getting out of bed, tell yourself: "I have to go to work—as a human being. What do I have to complain of, if I'm going to do what I was born for—the things I was brought into the world to do? Or is this what I was created for? To huddle under the blankets and stay warm?
>
> 'But it's nicer here...'
>
> So you were born to feel "nice"? Instead of doing things and experiencing them? Don't you see the plants, the birds, the ants and spiders and bees going about

their individual tasks, putting the world in order, as best they can? And you're not willing to do your job as a human being? Why aren't you running to do what your nature demands?

'—But we have to sleep sometime...'

Agreed. But nature set a limit on that—as it did on eating and drinking. And you're over the limit. You've had more than enough of that. But not of working. There you're still below your quota. You don't love yourself enough. Or you'd love your nature too, and what it demands of you. People who love what they do wear themselves down doing it, they even forget to wash or eat."

Grant Yourself Permission

Self-growth begins with the simple and profound act of being OK with who you are, right now. With this attitude, you face hardship calmly and with the ability to look forward instead of spiralling into negativity. Plus, you're likely to find more creative and harmonious ways out of those hardships than if you'd rigidly held on to how things were "supposed" to be.

Mental strength, resilience and unflappability are not traits of perfectionists and those who bully themselves. They belong to people who understand the power of self-compassion, and who can shift and adjust, forgiving mistakes, accepting what can't be changed with grace and composure. So, let's shift our focus from what we are at liberty to control and optimize, and consider one crucial thing that we *cannot* control:
We will all make mistakes; none of us is or can ever be perfect, no matter how hard we try.

Knowing this, it would be irrational to expect perfection, of ourselves or others. It would invite misery for no good reason.

And yet, just the thought of self-acceptance begs the question: Does that just mean being OK with being mediocre, with doing poorly in life and making no effort? Here, it's important to understand what compassionate self-acceptance is and isn't.

Giving yourself permission to be human doesn't mean planning to do poorly, but rather accepting the fact that sometimes you will fall short, no matter what you plan, and that's OK. Allowing for imperfection is not the same as striving for it. It's not at all the same thing as giving up, being apathetic, or living without values or hard work. It simply means that you ease up on yourself and acknowledge that there will be parts of your life that are messy, difficult, unpleasant or regrettable, even when you're trying your best. Rather than a license to do poorly, being accepting and self-compassionate is actually a way to ask more of yourself in the long run.

Reframe mistakes as a necessary cost of learning and improving. Embrace the opportunity to stumble and fail—it's one of the most powerful ways we learn and grow. Change is always possible, but it's seldom neat and easy. More often than not, it's slower than you'd like, occasionally embarrassing, and downright difficult. But being hard on yourself about your failures gets you nowhere. Only patient diligence and the willingness to disregard the occasional slip-up will get you there. Ultimately, the attitude of patience, temperance, forgiveness, compassion and resilience all comes down to a broad sentiment of "it's OK."

It's OK to Be Human

Humans are imperfect. It's not a bug, it's a feature. Embrace being in process—we are always on a path, and if we are willing to take risks, try new ideas, and fall on our faces occasionally, we can learn to trust that the path takes us where we need to go, even if some parts of the journey are rough. Those difficult parts teach us what we want, what we like, and what is bad for us. A new mother finds herself losing her temper one day with her baby, but rather than berating herself for not living a picture-perfect life 100 percent of the time, she takes a deep breath, forgives herself, and moves on.

It's OK to Mess Up

We are not our thoughts, and we are not even our actions. We have to take responsibility for them, sure, and ideally grow from them. But this doesn't mean people who make mistakes are bad people or unworthy ones. Give yourself permission to make mistakes—yes, even really big ones—and know that you're not more likely to improve just by being mean to yourself. Self-forgiveness is the fastest way to process and make good use of a slip-up, rather than dwelling in martyrdom or beating yourself up. It might make it easier to be kind to yourself if you remember that doing so helps you actually get on with the business of being better.

Only once you can get over the self-admonishment and shame, can you look objectively at how to do better next time round. If you've ever had someone wrong you and then try to apologize, you'll know that it's useless to hear how bad *they* feel about everything—what you really want to hear is their plan to make sure it never happens again!

It's OK to Fail

We live in a culture with an acute fear of failure. This is probably because we internalize our success and failures as parts of our identities—i.e., failing at an endeavor makes *you* a failure. Take the pressure off and remind yourself that success and failure are things that happen; they are not the be all and end all of who you are and don't determine your worth as a person. Rather than trying to eradicate the prospect of failure from your life entirely, try instead to increase the *quality* of the failures you make. You will always make mistakes, but you can attempt and fail at progressively more challenging tasks—proof that you're advancing and learning.

We tell our children that it's fine to fail, as long as they try again *and succeed the next time*. But what if you never do? Sometimes a failure doesn't occur because we didn't try hard enough or didn't persevere. Sometimes it's just because we're not cut out for a certain role or task, and our "failure" is really a helpful sign that we're in the wrong place, or have set unrealistic goals for ourselves. Failure can be an invitation to reassess our goals or the way we're approaching them.

It's OK to Feel Bad

Yes, calmly weathering life's challenges with grace and poise is the goal. Yes, we all want to develop resilience and grit. But deep self-compassion even extends to those occasions when we feel negative emotions, despite having loftier expectations of ourselves.

Counterintuitively, it's accepting the full gamut of human emotions that allows them to pass more quickly. It's possible to reframe experiences more positively, to be chipper about life, to take failure in your stride. But it's also good work to notice that you're feeling defeated, depressed or frustrated. It's completely normal to experience pain, anger or sadness. Denying these feelings will only cause them to fester inside, whereas acknowledging them allows us to learn from them and move on.

This bears repeating: negative emotions are not a problem to be fixed, they are simply passing events that can be embraced with acceptance or stubbornly resisted. Resisting them stubbornly, however, has a funny way of making them last longer.

It's OK to Feel Good

On the other hand, cultivating an accepting attitude and being compassionate with yourself also entails allowing yourself to feel good when you feel good. You have permission to enjoy your success, to feel lucky and blessed, to be proud of yourself or excited and hopeful for the future. You also have permission to feel that way despite any stories about what you "deserve" or what you need to have accomplished before celebrating. Feeling victorious, or enjoying the rewards of life is not something to be ashamed of or guard against.

Many workaholics unconsciously hold the belief that enjoying your life makes you a bad person; doing so implies you're resting on your laurels, rather than striving for something greater and continuing to work to improve. But emotions don't make us who we are, whether they're "positive" or "negative" ones. If someone compliments your success, try accepting it gracefully and enjoying the fruits of your hard work without playing it down or focusing on what you didn't do right.

It's OK to Be a Beginner

Feeling intolerant of the intermediate states of a learning process means we value the destination, but don't value the *process of getting there*. If you were watching a tiny baby learning to walk, would you feel inclined to say that every time the baby stumbled it had failed, and that something was wrong? Or would you merely smile, knowing that falling down often isn't a sign that learning is going wrong, but rather that it's going exactly how it should?

Everyone wants to evolve and improve, but this demands from us the courage to struggle a little, to try things we haven't done before, and do them when we're still unsure and unskilled. It's OK to be a beginner— experts are no more virtuous or valuable than beginners, they're merely at a different point on the same journey. You're not lazy; in fact, you're working harder by attempting a new challenge. You haven't failed. You are merely in process. Try to see obstacles as a given, and *expect* that things will be hard sometimes. You'll be better primed to face them when you do.

It's OK to Need Help

Reading much of the personal development literature out there, you could be forgiven for thinking that every human is a lone warrior in a hostile wilderness, trying to claw his way to the life he wants, with nothing but his own wits to help him. But here again it pays to forget about our egos for a moment and remember that we are social beings, and that interdependence with others is a part of our DNA. It's not a problem that we occasionally need help from one another (or need to give it!).

Every single successful person has a history of being held and supported by others, right back to their childhoods where their mothers carried, birthed, fed and loved them for years on end. All great people have had benefactors, teachers and role models. Even strong people occasionally need a morale-boosting talk with loved ones—in fact, their ability to seek and follow advice as well as embrace their vulnerability is part of what makes them strong.

Self-reliance, like perfectionism, is a trait better suited to machines than people. You don't have to go it alone. Use the resources around you and develop strong relationships with others where value is shared and exchanged for the benefit of everyone.

It's OK for Other People to Be Imperfect

This leads us neatly to one more aspect of developing patience, temperance and an attitude of compassionate acceptance. What the Buddhists call compassion is essentially the ability to let people be what they are, without judgment. Compassion for self and compassion for others are the same trait—one cannot be cultivated without the other. Being judgmental and harsh with others only makes it harder to be kind to yourself; likewise, we can see our attitudes toward our own failures reflected back at us when we respond to others' failures. It can be an enormous relief to allow those around you to make mistakes, to feel what they feel, to grow, to be imperfect—just as you are! In fact, in a profound way, embracing this humanity can pave the way for a deep form of love and compassion.

When you feel wronged by another, take a step back and deliberately choose to forgive them, to go easy. You don't have to be a saint—after all, your reactions are valid, too. However, it might be much easier in the long run, more productive and more pleasant to make room for the imperfections of others, without judging them for who they are and where they are on their journey. Being inflexible and overly critical doesn't help others any more than it helps yourself. If you can find the strength to rise above conflicts and disappointments with others, you may discover something more valuable than being right—you may cultivate a more resilient sense of self-worth that goes beyond the judgments of the ego.

Granting yourself the permission to be a fallible human changes your expectations.

Change Takes Vulnerability

Ever heard "no pain, no gain"? It's a platitude that comes from a mindset that sees change as a necessarily traumatic process. As a battle, even. We picture ourselves versus the world, valiantly and defiantly fighting against it, till we're the victorious winners at the top of the mountain. We imagine ourselves hunkering down and getting tough with ourselves, bracing against our own weakness, *forcing* the outcome we choose.

This attitude is a recipe for disaster. We're going to end this book by diving deep into the nuts and bolts of what change is actually is – and why it so seldom looks like what our culture teaches us to expect of transformation.

Let's begin by looking at the natural world and seeing how transformation occurs, whether that's over a single organism's lifespan or over thousands of years of evolutionary change. Look at how a plant or tree grows. You'll notice something: in plants, there is something rigid and static (standing still) and there is something alive and growing (moving). There is the tiny, soft and growing green bud that is new, fresh and flexible. And there's the old growth that is solid, hardened and tough. It's not growing anymore. It's more like "banked" growth.

Plants keep these two functions in dynamic balance – when the environment is filled with nutrients, the plant puts its energy into new growth into the leaves and stems, so it grows bigger. When times are tough it hunkers down and sends energy into the roots instead. It doesn't increase in size, but seeks to support the size it is. However, gardeners know that if plants grow too quickly, they can fail to develop a stable root system and topple over, even though they look nice and large and have plenty of flashy green leaves and flowers. On the other hand, plants can also be too stagnant – while they are stable and solid (and would make great firewood!) they are not growing or changing. They are not producing anything. They are just surviving – closer to dead than alive!

So, it comes down to the dynamic tension between two drives:

Expand or stabilize.
Explore or stay put.

Grow or stay the same.

So, what does this have to do with self-coaching? Well, humans, who are also living organisms, follow the same principle. We too can either move or stay still, expand or hunker down, grow or stay as we are. Since we are interested in the attitude required to transform and develop, let's look at this spirit of expansion, exploration and growth.

"Men are born soft and supple; dead they are stiff and hard. Plants are born tender and pliant; dead, they are brittle and dry. Thus, whoever is stiff and inflexible is a disciple of death. Whoever is soft and yielding is a disciple of life. The hard and stiff will be broken. The soft and supple will prevail." – Lao Tzu

This softness and suppleness are what characterize the growth mindset. Contrary to the "no pain, no gain" dogma, it suggests that growing things are flexible, yielding and curious, rather than forceful and stubborn. Death is invulnerable, certain, and fixed – life is more playful than that, and keeps things open-ended. Though this principle was already known to Lao Tzu and his contemporaries over 2500 years ago, the idea has cropped up in modern psychology and personal development spheres as the difference between "fixed mindset" and "growth mindset."

Psychologist Carol Dweck pinpointed the ideas, behaviors, thoughts, feelings and attitudes common to people who know how to learn, grow and develop… versus those that never do. Rather than a set of predictable behaviors, she identified the necessary attitude or mindset – in fact, a completely different way of seeing yourself and being in the world – that predicted success and transformation.

First, she identified the mindset *not* associated with growth, the **fixed mindset**:

- Intelligence, skill or capacity is seen as static and innate (i.e., fixed)
- Essentially, growth is not perceived as possible
- The focus is on what you *are* and not what you *do* (recall the difference between feedback and advice)

- Failure is taken personally and seen as unacceptable
- The response to an obstacle is to give up (why would you repeatedly try to do something you could never do anyway, and which made you feel bad?)
- Effort is seen as futile, and challenges are avoided
- Constructive feedback or advice is felt as painful or rejected
- Other people's success is experienced as threatening, so there is jealousy
- Mistakes result in blaming others or failing to take responsibility (after all, failure is shameful)
- Faced with change, the "hard and stiff are broken"

The **growth mindset** is the opposite:

- Intelligence, skill or capacity is seen as negotiable, changeable, and able to be improved
- Essentially, growth is seen as normal and expected
- The focus is on what you *do* and not what you *are*

- Failure is accepted as a valuable part of the learning and growing process
- The response to an obstacle is to become curious about possible ways around it
- Effort is seen as a given, and challenges are embraced
- Constructive feedback is considered without allowing it to reflect on your worth as a human being
- Other people's success is inspiring and a reason to celebrate
- Mistakes are accepted quickly and easily, without blame or shame
- Faced with change, the "soft and supple prevail"

Let's look at an example to show how these two mindsets play out in the world. Two people sign up for a pottery class after work every Thursday. Person A has always considered themselves an artistic sort, and they've been called "a natural" and "gifted" when it comes to painting and drawing. They secretly imagine that they'll be the star of the class, and see it as a platform to show everyone what they know. Person B is going along to the class because it looks fun, and they'd like to try out a relaxing new hobby. They can't even draw a stick man properly but they're willing to see what the teacher can show them!

In the first class, both person A and B make spectacular flops of their bowls. Person A is embarrassed by this and immediately gets defensive when the teacher starts giving pointers on how to make a better bowl next time. Person A is so angry and humiliated, they immediately argue with the teacher, assuming they are being unfairly criticized (*don't they know I'm a natural?*). They look at the other students' bowls and resent them – clearly, Person A just wasn't born with the pottery gene or something!

After the class, Person A is still fuming and tells Person B they won't go back, since there's no point. Pottery just isn't their thing, and besides the teacher doesn't like them. They strongly suspect that they failed because of the poor quality of the clay – and who would want to take lessons from a teacher who knows nothing about the right clay?

Person B is confused when they hear this – who said anything about *failing*? The way they see it, they're both beginners and don't know how to do pottery yet – that's why they're taking the class! They never expected perfection, and they never had any big Pottery Ego to get dented. Person B returns to the class the next week, and implements the tips the teacher gave. Their bowl is a little better now. Not as good as another student's, but then they ask that student for advice and try to emulate their technique in the third class.

By the end of the year, Person B has mastered bowls and now knows how to make cups and jugs, too, and they're busy refining their glazing technique. They have their first misshapen bowl proudly on display in the living room. It's a hilarious talking piece, but Person B also likes to see it so they can be reminded of how far they've come. Person A, never having returned, knows nothing more about pottery than they did in that first lesson. Their bowl went into the trash.

The interesting thing is this: Person A genuinely did embark on the journey with more raw artistic talent than Person B. But they also brought with them the worst possible attitude to the process.

What's more, both Person A and B experienced the same initial "failure" – it was merely their response to this that made the difference. The stiff and inflexible, even when it is superior in other ways, still cannot beat the soft and supple when it comes to the game of change. Person B laughs and says, "Oh, pottery is just something I play around with every week. I'm still a beginner." And therein is the irony: the more they feel themselves a beginner, the more mastery they cultivate.

The Ego Can Jeopardize Growth

You cannot get better if you are desperately clinging to yours being perfect already.
You cannot learn something new if you cannot admit that you don't already know everything.

And you cannot become an expert at anything unless you are first willing to be a novice.

In other words, you cannot grow and be stagnant simultaneously!

To grow into something new, you have to leave the old behind. To get bigger than you are right now, you need to fully accept and acknowledge all the ways you are currently small! This takes special courage – the courage to be soft, supple and vulnerable. The desire to be right, to know everything, to be certain, to be secure, to be solid – we cannot stay in this state of mind *and* grow, because growth requires moving into new places we haven't already explored. And there is a certain risk in that.

The ego can play a terrible trick on us, especially if the desire for change and growth comes straight from the ego. We may picture our development in terms of the finished outcome only, where our self-esteem is bolstered, and we are feeling proud and invulnerable (and maybe better than everyone else). We like the *feeling of mastery* – of being in control of the world, of ourselves, and our abilities – but not the process of developing that mastery. This is precisely why we feel so terrible when we try to learn something new and instead of enjoying that mastery and sense of control, we only encounter our incompetence and lack of skill. We look at the big distance between that lofty goal and where we are now, and get discouraged. It can feel embarrassing, overwhelming, or pointless to keep trying. We give up and look for easier goals!

But all those people who do possess mastery (or insight, success, happiness or any other goal you can identify) began from the same place as you did – in a state where they possessed none of the desired quality, and were far, far away from the endpoint. From a fixed mindset, we might imagine those people are just lucky or talented. We picture them being born with everything they need, and we, not being as fortunate, can never do as they do. The real difference may be those people never saw themselves as talented or lucky at all – and knew that they had to work hard if they wanted to reach their goal! This is why you sometimes see people who were called "gifted" in childhood ultimately fail in life – they were never taught what to do in the face of (inevitable) challenges or mistakes. Since their identity is bound up in being intelligent, they cannot endure any sensation of feeling unintelligent. So, they avoid every situation that makes them feel that way – i.e., the entire realm of learning!

Behavior change can only happen when accompanied by the right shift in attitude. We grow, learn and develop when we are soft and supple of mind, when we let go of the defensiveness of the ego, and when we will be humble and patient on the path to our goals. A marathon is finished in the final step – but most of your effort will be required to take the thousands of steps that come *before* that one. You cannot take one step, and then give up because you are not instantly rewarded with the feeling you expect on completing the final step.

The ego and the fixed mindset go hand in hand. You'll know that you're in this mindset if you frame effort, obstacle and failure in personal terms, as though they say something about you as a human. Often, a passive and nihilistic approach to life results from never seeing yourself as capable of real transformation. When the ego is running the show, your objectivity also takes a knock, because you overidentify with everything, and cannot step back and look at your efforts for what they are.

How does it get better? How do we keep our ego in check and adopt a growth mindset?

Well, in keeping with the spirit of things, it's not a case of "you either have it or you don't"! It's 100% something that can be learnt, with time and consistency. Here are a few exercises and techniques to cultivate a growth mindset in yourself.

Technique 1: Seek out failure

Yikes. Really? Seek out failure?

Well, the idea is to desensitize yourself to making mistakes, and view them less as a threat to the ego and more an everyday part of being alive. Failure is not a detour from success – it's what the road to success is made of! You can counter fixed mindset thinking by deliberately seeking imperfection, instead of fearfully avoiding it. This may seem scary, but it permits you to just learn without performing and being perfect the first time around. It lowers the stakes and takes the pressure off. The more you fail, and the more you teach yourself to interpret that failure is no big deal, the less likely you are to let momentary discomforts derail your progress.

- One good habit: laugh at yourself. Often. Mistakes are not the end of the world. You look like a fool for at least 6 months as you learn swing dancing – so what? Does looking like a fool stop you from having fun or learning? Does it threaten anything at all?
- Another thing to try is to attempt something with no expectation you will "win." Just try it for practice, or to learn more. Drop the goal and make your own mission to handle what's in front of you at the moment. This is the attitude that makes engineers say, "Hmm, that didn't work. I'm going to make a change and try it again, to see if *that* works." They are not

attached to either outcome, since if it works or doesn't work it still yields valuable information. The process of learning is what's important.
- Take an interest in those people you consider failures. What can you learn from them?
- Finally, forget about "taking risks." Let go of the outcome and deliberately choose an activity you *know* you won't succeed at. Then, just play around with it. You have nothing to prove! Don't rush. You may find you are actually more creative bumbling through on your own than when you're trying to force yourself to follow some pre-defined path.

Technique 2: Reframe what it means to be challenged

Our attitudes are reflected in the language we choose. But our language can also affect how we think and feel, reinforcing those attitudes. Sometimes, all it takes to shift your mindset is to change the way you talk about things.

- Make a habit of saying "yet." As long as you are alive, you are in the process. You are not finished. So, watch your language and say things like, "I haven't figured out how to do that yet" or "I'm still working on this!" instead of closing things off prematurely by saying, "Ugh, I don't know how to do this" or "this isn't right." Remember that judgment kills objectivity and takes you out of the moment. It's OK to be halfway to a goal.
- Don't talk about who you are, talk about what you do. When you shift the focus away from yourself, you can put it on concrete actions out in the world – and it's far easier to change these actions than to change who you are at your core. So, you don't say, "I'm an average piano player" but "I'm currently doing my grade 4 piano."
- Instead of using words like "problem," choose less judgmental and fixed-sounding words like "situation," challenge," "task" or simply "what's happening." Saying, "we're looking for ways to upgrade the heating in this building" is more neutral than saying, "we have a bad heating problem in this

place." A problem suggests an unmovable obstacle. A task is just something you're in the process of sorting out. It's more objective. Using words like "opportunity" to describe a situation not going your way may seem cheesy, but it immediately opens your perception to new possibilities.

- As we saw in the section on non-judgmental observation, we can drop the habit of labeling things or making value judgments, and just see them with objectivity and curiosity. Sometimes we jump in to say that something is wrong just because it's unexpected or new. But what if the unexpected or unwanted thing is better than what we were anticipating? Even if you can only say of a challenging time that it was "interesting," you are still using a little humor – which is a very sophisticated form of resilience!

The growth mindset, or what Lao Tzu calls being supple, is shown in our attitude towards challenge, effort, and the discomfort of change. If we yield to learning, and stay flexible, we give ourselves the chance to actually become more than what we are now. If we put or ego first and stubbornly resist challenge, effort and discomfort, we get to keep our pride and certainty, but we stay as we are. The choice is simple: we can have our egos... or we can take the risk of growing, learning, changing and becoming *better* than our egos.

Summary:

- Growth, self-awareness and objectivity are less about specific actions and more about attitude. One way to turn the improvement journey on its head is not to ask what you'd most like in life, but for what you will suffer. This reorients you to the inevitable hard work and challenge that comes with lasting change and makes it more likely that you will stay the course.
- Contrary to what our culture teaches us, change takes vulnerability, openness, humility and flexibility rather than stubborn determination and force. Carol Dweck's "fixed mindset" sees characteristics as innate and unchangeable, and with this attitude, we avoid challenge, take failure personally,

and resist effort. We are less resilient and more ego-driven – and we also don't reach our goals.
- The "growth mindset" sees the self as capable of development and improvement, and consequently, challenges are embraced. This is a focus on what you do rather than what you are, and is an attitude most associated with genuine change.
- The ego can jeopardize efforts at growth. If we are intolerant of uncertainty, unable to own up to mistakes or if we see our performance as part of our identity, we will resist the learning process and give up too easily. We cannot be mentally "supple" enough to be open to new experiences because we prefer to be right and in control. This is ultimately self-defeating.
- We can counter ego-driven attitudes by deliberately seeking failure in life and becoming not just resilient to it, but appreciative of its power to teach us. We can also practice reframing how we look at challenge, obstacle or failure by tweaking our language. This way, we can keep our minds open to potential

opportunities and solutions, rather than prematurely shutting down perception.

Summary Guide

CHAPTER 1. FRAMEWORKS FOR CHANGE

- A coach facilitates our growth process, but that doesn't mean we cannot coach ourselves. With self-awareness, a framework for change, the right tools, and the ability to be objective about our progress, we can help ourselves achieve our goals.
- Change occurs when we move from Point A to Point B. There are many ways to cover that distance, but you'll need a framework to help you organize yourself.
- One useful model of change is the coaching model called GROW, in which the letters spell Goals (what do I want?), Reality (what is happening right now?), Options (what could I do?) and Will (what will I do?). We will see these essential steps repeated all throughout the remainder of the book.

- Another model is the Outcome Frame model, which asks us to take concrete steps towards achieving our Desired State, i.e., goal.
- Step 1: Identify what you want. Define your Desired State. We identify what we want, and understand the benefits of that change, and the criteria for measuring its success. We also consider all the obstacles to our achieving this goal, and iron out the exact details and context. Finally, we end in a comparable way to the GROW model: we take concrete action.
- There is no right or wrong framework, but the GROW model may work better for professional or external goals, whereas The Outcome Frame model may be better for more personal or relationship goals.

CHAPTER 2. KNOW YOURSELF, GROW YOURSELF

- To know the goals we should set, we need to know more about who we are and

what we value. Self-knowledge is a prerequisite for growth.
- There are many ways to learn more about yourself. One way is the Wheel of Life, which divides our being into 8 key areas. By carefully mapping out a pie chart showing how we rate each area on a scale of 1 to 10, we can see at a glance our relative satisfaction with each area. This can inform the goals we set for ourselves, for example by seeing where we are unbalanced or lacking.
- Another self-knowledge tool is to think of your life in terms of how well you are meeting the 6 basic human needs, most commonly understood to be love and connection, variety, significance, certainty, growth and contribution. There are healthy and unhealthy ways to meet these needs. We can create the most impactful goals by seeing which of our needs are not going met, or which are being met in an unhealthy way. We can ask: what is my need right now and what's the healthiest way to meet that need?
- Effective goal-setting can also come from knowledge of one's deepest personal

values and principles. Knowing what is most important to you – service, creativity, independence, etc. – will help you shape the goals that are most appropriate for your unique life.
- If you're not sure what your values are in life, don't worry; discovering them is not hard. However, the process does take time, and you won't simply wake up tomorrow with complete knowledge of what your values are.
- The first step to discovering what your values are is to simply abandon all preconceived notions you have of who you are. Often, the values we have been living by are actually derived externally. This can be through our family, culture, historical era, etc. By starting from a clean slate, we avoid such influences from clouding our judgment regarding our true values.
- Next, think about the things that you feel most strongly about. This could be personal success, close family bonds, serving others in the form of social work, etc. Finding one will often lead you to other values you hold because they point to a "higher" value you possess. Thus,

valuing family over career means that your interpersonal relationships in general are valuable to you.
- One final technique is to actively visualize your future self, living your best life, once all goals are accomplished. This can help you see new solutions, excite you about possibilities, and connect you to what you desire. Just remember to anchor any insights you have into reality by taking concrete steps towards those goals.

CHAPTER 3. THE POWER OF OBJECTIVITY

- Objectivity is an essential skill on the path to being your own coach, since it allows you to step out of your perceptions and see them from a distance, rather than getting identified and entangled with them. The best way to gain more self-awareness is to be curious and ask questions – in the first place, we should be aware of our subjectivity and realize that our perception differs from reality.

- The best way to gain self-awareness is to ask about your behaviors and actions, not your intentions or thoughts. Your thoughts are too easily corrupted or otherwise simply not representative of what you actually feel. When you can analyze your behaviors and actions, you can then glean real information about yourself.
- There are several questions you can ask yourself. For example, what is one achievement that you're most proud of and one thing you've done that you're most ashamed of? The achievement you're proud of will reveal a lot about what you value, and what kind of skills you are good at that made the achievement possible in the first place. On the other hand, the thing you're ashamed of is something you should be wary about repeating and reminding yourself that you do not want to be the same person who did that horrible thing.
- Judgment hinders clear and objective perception. We judge from a position of fear or a need for control or certainty, but it's a skill to perceive things as they are,

without assigning values, narratives or interpretations.
- We can gain more objectivity by comparing our perception against other people's when we ask for advice (which is better than asking for feedback, since it centers on the task and not you personally). We need to pick people whose perception we trust, and ask the right questions, and be prepared to take on what they say without ego and defensiveness.
- The Johari window technique is a great way to compare how we see ourselves with how others see us. We want to learn what others can see in us which we can't.
- The right question depends on the stage of the journey you're on. Initially, you can ask clarity questions to refine goals, then purpose questions to figure out your values and real desires. Challenge questions help you clarify your approach to setbacks and difficulties, while "getting unstuck" questions are there to get you moving again when you're lacking motivation, clarity or insight.

CHAPTER 4. ATTITUDE IS DESTINY

- Growth, self-awareness and objectivity are less about specific actions and more about attitude. One way to turn the improvement journey on its head is not to ask what you'd most like in life, but for what you will suffer. This reorients you to the inevitable hard work and challenge that comes with lasting change and makes it more likely that you will stay the course.
- Contrary to what our culture teaches us, change takes vulnerability, openness, humility and flexibility rather than stubborn determination and force. Carol Dweck's "fixed mindset" sees characteristics as innate and unchangeable, and with this attitude, we avoid challenge, take failure personally, and resist effort. We are less resilient and more ego-driven – and we also don't reach our goals.
- The "growth mindset" sees the self as capable of development and improvement, and consequently, challenges are embraced. This is a focus

on what you do rather than what you are, and is an attitude most associated with genuine change.
- The ego can jeopardize efforts at growth. If we are intolerant of uncertainty, unable to own up to mistakes or if we see our performance as part of our identity, we will resist the learning process and give up too easily. We cannot be mentally "supple" enough to be open to new experiences because we prefer to be right and in control. This is ultimately self-defeating.
- We can counter ego-driven attitudes by deliberately seeking failure in life and becoming not just resilient to it, but appreciative of its power to teach us. We can also practice reframing how we look at challenge, obstacle or failure by tweaking our language. This way, we can keep our minds open to potential opportunities and solutions, rather than prematurely shutting down perception.

www.ingramcontent.com/pod-product-compliance
Lightning Source LLC
Chambersburg PA
CBHW020531080526
44583CB00013B/815